Murray's
Cabaret Club

BEAK STREET,
REGENT STREET, W 1

First published 2019

The History Press
The Mill, Brimscombe Port
Stroud, Gloucestershire, GL5 2QG
www.thehistorypress.co.uk

British Library Cataloguing in Publication Data.
A catalogue record for this book is available from the British
Library.

ISBN 978 0 7509 9132 2

Design by Katie Beard
Printed in Turkey by Imak

Murray's Cabaret Club

BEAK STREET,
REGENT STREET, W1

DISCOVERING
SOHO'S SECRET

BENJAMIN LEVY

FOREWORD BY DITA VON TEESE

CONTENTS

FOREWORD

by Dita Von Teese

Is it any wonder that today's showgirl enthusiasts, including yours truly, are mad about the myth of Murray's? Extravagant floorshows, extravagant costumes and extravagant carousing were all in a late-night's work for the showgirls of Murray's Cabaret Club, the landmark London venue that dominated the mid-century afterhours of many a bold-faced prince, politician and personality.

Its scandalous history between one of its young dancers and a conservative politician notwithstanding, Murray's would undeniably remain a source of legend and fascination to this day. For 'Pops', as founder Percy Murray was known to his army of skilled performers, seamstresses, lyricists, waiters, hostesses, cooks and others employed in this precision operation – he employed upwards of 130 to see to the maximum nightly guests of 110 – everything from the dancers' lacquered nails to the polished wood walls mattered. As the creative director of my own burlesque revue, I can get behind Pops' mission to deliver a lavish, over-the-top experience worth more than the price of admission.

But I also find kinship in Murray's 'Girls', as the showgirls came to be known. These young hopefuls from duller corners of the country came to London for the excitement and found it at this famed club, with its unassuming front

door tucked away off Beak Street. In press releases and newspaper columns, a rising star would be touted as 'more than a pretty face', her interest in sports, academics and even wartime efforts part of the story. No prior dance experience or instruction needed to apply. Yet they sure underwent a rigorous audition and instruction to stay there. Performers would bank much more than they had in their previous gigs as typists and shop girls, so even a brief taste each night of spotlights and sparkle was worth the hours of rehearsal and requisite weekly visits to the salon. I, thankfully, wrote my own ticket – and that includes not having to endure the casting couch like some of these women did with Pops. But as a dishwater blonde from the Midwest who has not so much reinvented as realized my true self by way of a strong work ethic, determination and barrels of Swarovski crystals, I can relate to their desires.

Jean Harlow, a reinvention in her own right, was among Murray's storied female fans, even years before Princess Margaret was a regular at the club. And respectable wives and fiancées, clad in their chicest, accompanied many of the members on weekends, on what Pop's called 'family night'. Of course, the patrons – vetted members and their equally vetted friends – didn't only cram into the subterranean club to grab a steak and martini before last call at 1 a.m. It was all about the floorshow. And it was literally on the floor, just inches from the celebrated guests. A choreographer, lighting engineer and live band were among the many on the payroll. Two shows nightly, each of the trio of dancing acts more glamorously and provocatively costumed than the previous number. Fringe and fishnets, ruffles and rhinestones, top hats and even topless torsos dazzled audiences.

To wit, for me, it's all about the costumes! Some of the most masterful costume designers of the time – who happened to hone their talents in the world of London's luxe cabaret clubs, as well as storied theatre stages – contributed inspired, elaborate concoctions. At Murray's, no expense was spared, and designers such as Hilda Wetton, Ronald Cobb and Michael Bronze delivered. There were headdresses suggesting birdcages, with a vivid faux bird perched on a dancer's shoulder; an oval frame resembling a rainbow that the dancer would clutch, a tuft of fluffy clouds concealing her nether regions; a black robe speckled in large white musical notes giving way to nothing more than sheer striped opera gloves and a tiny violin at the navel, strapped around

Dita Von Teese,
Photograph by
Franz Szony

her waist with lavish backside bows. No topic was off limits, from Medieval history to surrealist art, perfume counter girls to police officers.

The art of the tease was taking place nightly among the clientele and staff alike in this intimate jewel box of a club, electric with seduction, secrets and society, high and low. While Murray's closed when I was scarcely out of grade school, I've had the pleasure to work and play in such a milieu as both a guest and guest star at Le Crazy Horse de Paris, an extraordinary institution in its own right since 1951, with an equally storied and celebrated patronage.

How I wish we had Murray's now, to visit and perform in! At least we have this volume to hold, honouring the dreams of the talented individuals who kept Murray's in the spotlight as long as they did. I hope it inspires you to conjure your own myths as it does for me.

Dita Von Teese
April 2019

ACKNOWLEDGEMENTS

It takes a strong eye and a seasoned collector to spot a treasure trove, and I thank art dealer Charlie Jeffreys for bringing this wonderful collection of cabaret ephemera to my attention. Thank you also to Tony Shrimplin from the Museum of Soho for engineering a superb exhibition on Murray's Cabaret Club, and improving the public's engagement with the broader subject of the West End's rich history of entertainment. A big thank you to Dita Von Teese for her enthusiasm and insightful foreword.

My gratitude also goes to Jean Hendy-Harris, Iris Chapple and Teena Symonds for their memories; Michelene Wandor for her careful reading of the manuscript; Geoff Marsh and Vicky Broackes from the V&A for all their guidance and permission to access and photograph their archives; Rachel Levy for her wonderful photography; Luci Gosling and everyone from the Mary Evans Picture Library for their work on the illustrations; Seymour Platt; Jenny Murray and her family; Rick Dalgleish; Barry Miles; James Birch; Patrick Bogue; Getty Images; the Century Club; the British Film Institute; and British Pathé.

Finally, thank you to my publishers, The History Press, for taking on this project and producing such a lavish book.

I

HISTORY

Working at Murray's left you in an unreal world: at night-time you entered this fantasy place, where the rich and famous queued for your attention; the days were an endless series of dinner and party invitations, and the social life was truly amazing. It was only after I left Murray's and returned to the real world that I realised the strange underground fantasy life I had been leading.

Christine Keeler[1]

Lewis Morley's now-iconic photograph of Christine Keeler, taken at the height of the Profumo Affair. 1963
© Lewis Morley Archive/Seymour Platt

... and so it was that night after night, Murray's Cabaret Club set imaginations ablaze, forged fantasies for deadened aristocrats, served a dish of dreams to Arab businessmen and provided refuge for the hounded celebrity. In that intimate basement beneath the pavements of Soho's Beak Street, sexy was never sordid, and nude never naked.

But the make-believe spell was broken in 1963, when a sex-and-spying scandal erupted; it was revealed that showgirl Christine Keeler had been sleeping with the Conservative Minister of War, John Profumo. Keeler was a teenage runaway who had joined Murray's in 1959. There she had met favoured customer Stephen Ward, a friend of the boss's son, David Murray. Ward was a supremely well-connected society osteopath. He was also a procurer of beautiful women, whom he inducted into his high society network. He soon whisked working-class Keeler off to his friend Lord Astor's parties

Stephen Ward, the osteopath charged with living off the profits of prostitution, pictured soon before he committed suicide. 1963
© Marx Memorial Library/Mary Evans Picture Library

at Cliveden, a grand country estate in Buckinghamshire. At one of these, the 19-year-old Keeler met 46-year-old John Profumo and they embarked on a sexual relationship. Profumo was married to the actress Valerie Hobson, though it was not his affair with Keeler that sparked press headlines across the nation. No one could have anticipated that Keeler was simultaneously bedding a Soviet spy masquerading as a businessman: Captain Yevgeny Ivanov. No-one, that is, but Ward, who had orchestrated this clandestine love triangle. He had introduced Ivanov and Keeler at a Cliveden pool party.

Conservative MP
John Profumo
with his wife,
Valerie Hobson.
c.1960
© *Illustrated
London News*/
Mary Evans
Picture Library

Lest we forget, these years in the early 1960s saw the height of the Cold War; the Cuban Missile Crisis encapsulated it and the Bond movies fictionalised it. A fear of Soviet espionage gripped the nation and the Profumo Affair became a national scandal – who knew what state secrets were being leaked between the bedsheets? The crisis only deepened in 1963 when a group of MPs from the Labour opposition alleged the impropriety of Profumo's supposed affair with Keeler, and, more worryingly, the risk to national security posed by Keeler's own affair with the spy Ivanov, who now had a direct link to a senior government minister. Profumo lied to Parliament by denying the impropriety of his actions and eventually resigned, though the tawdry play of events between the politician and his showgirl had an irreversible effect.

It dented national confidence in the prime minister, Harold Macmillan, and led to the subsequent downfall of the Conservative government. The defeat of the Establishment heralded the advent of a more permissive society, as the monochrome 1950s gave way to the technicolour '60s. London was swaying if not yet 'swinging'. That the Profumo Affair still fascinates today is borne out by the attention it continues to receive in the press, in museum exhibitions and on stage and screen.

The Profumo Affair was the stuff of cold hard political reality, contrasting with Murray's brand of finely choreographed escapism, life topped by a golden halo. This catalogue, and its accompanying exhibition, tells *that* story: the tale of the exotic Murray's Cabaret Club. It presents unpublished facts, figures and illustrations that aim to correct the many mistruths that linger about the club's legacy. The hope is that this unique institution's place in the history of British entertainment might be secured on its own terms.

The Good Old Days

The early history of Murray's Cabaret Club is complicated. Though it was founded in the early 1930s by a Percival Murray, it was never actually named *after* him. Rather, it emerged from the remnants of two previous nightclubs: Murray's Club and The Cabaret Club.

Murray's Club dates back to 1913. One of the earliest nightclubs established in London, it opened in response to a demand for places to dance the tango, the newly imported craze that was then sweeping through the West End. Jack May, an American who had worked in New York's nightclubs, founded the club and named it 'Murray's' after a sensationally luxurious restaurant-cum-dancehall back home on Broadway. Photographs and film footage from the 1920s and '30s show that his Soho club, which was on the corner of Beak Street and Regent Street, was equally extravagant A striking stairway descended to a cavernous ballroom, which was later expanded to include an American cocktail bar, all illuminated by Art Deco uplighters and mirrored pillars. Yet this was not all that Jack May borrowed from the club's American

cousin. From 1920, he introduced a short cabaret act that took place before dancing commenced. Cabaret had never really caught on in England, but it was all the rage in New York's 'rooftop garden clubs'. The Ziegfeld Follies popularised it in America, having borrowed it from Paris's Folies Bergère.

By contrast, The Cabaret Club was on Noel Street, not far from Murray's. It was founded in 1923, not long after *The Times* had reported that 'cabaret entertainments that are a feature of life on the Continent and in America are rapidly becoming more popular in London.'[2] 'Montmartre in London', proclaimed the *Sunday Post*.[3] However, The Cabaret Club did not share the success of Murray's, for its manager was a theatrical impresario called, coincidentally, Percival Murray, whose inexperience and bad fortune had almost driven it to the brink of bankruptcy. Murray, whose acting ambitions were scuppered by a war injury, had produced a few cabaret revues since 1919. One of these starred a young, unknown Gertrude Lawrence before she was poached, incidentally, by Jack May's club and turned into a star of the stage and screen.[4] The result: Percival Murray was dismissed in 1924 and, in 1926, Jack May's growing nightclub empire took control of The Cabaret Club in addition to Murray's.

As for Percival Murray, he ran off to Belgium to try his luck at the nightlife scene there. It was just as well, for scandal after scandal was just about hitting every nightclub under Jack May's aegis. The otherwise respectable veneer of Murray's – whose 'severe frontage [is] reminiscent of a bank or other staid and important business office'[5] – was blighted by rumours of supposedly demure young ladies snorting white powders off the smooth-surfaced glass dance floor. As far back as 1915, Jack May had been accused of introducing opium to the actress Billie Carleton. Her death in 1918 from an overdose shook the public's faith in the supposed moral

Billie Carleton (right) with Jack May, who introduced the tragic actress to opium. 1915
© *Illustrated London News / British Library*

health of a nation whose physical strength had been sapped by the Great War. Carleton's fate foreshadowed the advent of the fast and loose-living 1920s flapper, the only difference being the latter's drug of choice: cocaine. At The Cabaret Club, things were no better. Violence was the essence of its own racy underbelly; altercations on the dance floor between seemingly humdrum financiers and aristocrats were all too commonplace.

Predictably, matters came to a head in 1929. Jack May was implicated in a major corruption case involving the 'Queen of Soho' Kate Meyrick, who was bribing police to stave off raids on her own clubs. Jack May, who was doing the same at Murray's Club and The Cabaret Club, was ordered to leave the country. The press dubbed him a national disgrace and The Cabaret Club lost its licence, with Murray's Club reduced to a mere 'members' concern'.[6]

A New Start

London nightlife was now at a low ebb; it was no rival to the ecstasies of Bohemian Paris or the decadence of Weimar Berlin. Percival Murray recognised that serious competitors had dropped out of the race, and a power vacuum had arisen. The time was ripe for a return from the Continent, which he did in the early 1930s. He was now no longer handicapped by inexperience. He had run successful clubs and theatres in Brussels and Paris, and was ready to pioneer a new venture in London. This took the form of another nightclub, one that combined the striking revues of the old Cabaret Club with the brand name and members list of the old Murray's Club. Capitalising on the fortunate circumstance of his surname, Percival called it Murray's Cabaret Club and it was situated in the basement of 16–18 Beak Street, on the corner of Upper John Street, opposite the original Murray's Club.

Murray's Cabaret Club was far more exciting than any previous attempts at cabaret in London. This is because it introduced a phenomenon Percival Murray had witnessed in Paris: the 'cabaret floorshow'. The format typically meant scantily, though artfully, dressed showgirls performing in themed revues until early morning, with excellent dining in an intimate setting. The milieu was usually sophisticated and interactive; glamorous hostesses might work the room, chatting directly with the clientele.

Percival Murray's nightclub shattered the fourth wall with similar style. Every night at 10 p.m. and 1 a.m., he presented a floorshow that comprised three 'numbers'. These were dance routines based on a variety of themes: types of flowers, exotic countries, colourful sweets, styles of porcelain and so on. It was less a display of individual talent than, in the words of nightlife correspondent and future editor of *The Stage* Peter Hepple, 'Percival Murray's glamorous army' of women who collectively championed an extremely high standard of performance.[7] The troupe of forty-five dancers, soubrettes and showgirls was the 'largest line-up', Hepple deduced, 'of any nightspot in Europe, save possibly the Paris Lido'.[8] As many as twenty-five girls might be on the floor at any one time. Since the room was always packed and the club of bijou dimensions, former dancers can still recall having to skilfully

A floorshow
during dinner
at Murray's
Cabaret Club.
1956
© Hulton-
Deustch/Corbis/
Getty

dodge the toes of the seated patrons whilst performing. Not all of them were dancers. Most were showgirls who simply paraded the floor in staggeringly opulent costumes, illustrating the theme of the particular number. Nor were all the elaborately costumed girls part of the show. Some were hostesses whose services could be bought for a guinea each. They would be peppered amongst the audience, chatting to and drinking champagne with unaccompanied male customers.

Between each floorshow number, variety acts – conjurors, comedians, acrobats and the like – would perform. There was also dancing to two bands, one playing Latin American and the other more traditional dance music. Dinner was served from 8 p.m. to 1 a.m., followed by breakfast until 3 or 4 a.m.

Second World War

Business boomed at Murray's Cabaret Club during the Second World War. That the club was subterranean gave it a natural advantage, since it meant that the entertainment could safely continue during air raids. Increasingly, the mainstream press shone a spotlight onto various aspects of this unusual nightspot. Hostess Eunice Allman, 23, was one of the first employees to be profiled. The *Daily Express* in 1939 described how this 'great big, graceful healthy girl' with a 'husky voice' worked until 4 a.m. every day, 'soothing the bruised egos of restless business men'. Eunice apparently enjoyed conversing with her wealthy clients, 'subjects can range between big game fishing and a new drainage system in Bolivia'. Come 3 a.m., the article continued, the client usually asked Eunice whether she might move on somewhere else with him. At this point, 'Eunice can say, without a word of a lie: I'm sorry, but the management don't allow me to leave before 4.30.' Though most gentlemen were happy to pay £2 for her company, and some weeks she earned more than £20, Eunice said that clients often 'behave in an ill-bred manner … They are apt to stand on the table and sing, and they insist on buying dolls for all the girls.'[9]

Most profiles on individual employees highlighted their contribution to the war effort with jingoistic fervour. 'Warden and Croonette' ran one feature on Trixie Scales, an air-raid warden by day and singer at night.[10] Another article in *The Tatler* reported that 'delightful blonde' fan dancer Denise Vane was dutifully doing her own part as an air-raid warden, 'looking after a lucky section of Westminster's citizens'.[11] Some stories were deeply poignant. Singer and dancer Carole Kenyon came home one day to find her house wrecked by an air-raid bomb and her mother dead. She was due to perform that night at Murray's, and apparently did so without fuss. 'Carole is bringing happiness to people despite her great sorrow,' ran a feature in the *Daily Mirror*. 'She is a wonderful example to us all.'[12]

Shaking Things Up

Gambling dens, clip joints and other dubious rackets were, at this time, the stuff of Soho nightlife. Most existed only to fuel the demand for out-of-hours drinking; strict licensing laws prohibited drinking after 11 p.m. In order to dodge the restrictions, Murray's Cabaret Club was run on a 'bottle party system'. Clients signed a chit that enabled them to drink alcohol previously ordered but not paid for. In the wake of the Second World War, the licensing authorities tried to outlaw bottle party clubs and Percival Murray's livelihood was again in jeopardy.

In response to the consequent threat of closure, operations were stream-lined in the early 1950s, and a strict hierarchy of staff firmly established in order to legitimise Murray's as an institution. At the top was Percival Murray, founder and active president. Beneath him was 'Head Boy' David Murray, who was now the general manager, responsible for day-to-day logistics. He soon masterminded a complex acoustic and lighting system and installed a stage of illuminated glass. The 'Head Girl' was usually the principal dancer and chore-ographer. The inaugural holder of that post was Laurel Grey, who danced at Murray's from 1940. By the 1950s, she was producing her own floorshows and writing original lyrics to the numbers. Her successor in the 1960s was Doreen Dale, herself a dancer promoted to the executive echelons.

Every component of the floorshows was now brought in-house. Original lyrics were set to original music composed and orchestrated by the club's current bandleader. Original costumes were created by imaginative design-ers in collaboration with wardrobe mistress Elsie Burchmore. She and her team of seamstresses created the costumes from a shed on Percival Murray's country estate in Surrey. The seamstresses were employed full-time because new numbers were constantly in the works; new routines took a year to pre-pare and were changed with greater frequency than in any other floorshow in London.

Murray's Cabaret Club was now entering its heyday. From the 1950s onwards, it became a strong competitor to other popular London nightspots like the Pigalle, the Eve, Churchill's, L'Hirondelle, the Astor and the Stork. For sure, many nightclubs staged some sort of floorshow at the time. Few,

Percival Murray (left) with David Murray.
Late 1950s
© Rachel Levy/
Benjamin Levy

The seamstresses at work, with wardrobe mistress Elsie Burchmore in the background. 1956
© Cabaret Girl/ British Film Institute

Floorshow producer Laurel Grey dancing at Murray's in a costume designed by Ronald Cobb. 1946
© Trinity Mirror/ Mirrorpix/Alamy

however, were so inspired as the entertainments offered within Percival Murray's powerfully unique milieu. Even fewer employed the astronomical number of staff that he did – over 100; major West End theatres were employing little more than that for big musicals in the 1950s. There was a running joke in the press that Murray's was the club where the staff practically outnumbered the customers. In 1954, drama critic Youngman Carter reported from an exclusive behind-the-scenes tour of the club. He likened it to a 'luxurious if eccentric submarine, for every millimetre of the air-conditioned space is utilised in some ingenious way … cooks' galleys, lighting panels, changing rooms, store rooms and offices'.[13] As for the dressing rooms, another journalist thought that they were so large, beautifully panelled and expensively decorated that 'plenty of hotels … could take a tip or two from their comfort'.[14] The aim was to provide a sensational service that distinguished Murray's from any rival and, to that end, Percival Murray ran it with an iron fist; a stringent discipline was administered, 'convent-like', according to the recollections of former dancer Teena Symonds.

Offences included lateness, missing a cue, taking time off without permission, forgetting to wear nail varnish, missing the weekly visit to the hairdresser and failing to cover up patches left by swimsuit straps after sunbathing.

Making the Cut

'The line-up changes constantly as the girls are snapped up by agents and impresarios for bigger opportunities in the theatre and films. So Mr Murray is always on the look-out for replacements.' In fact, this 1954 advertisement continued, 'one vacancy occurs every ten days for an ambitious girl with talent and good looks.'[15] A year later, the *Daily Herald* informed readers that Percival Murray had just finished a round of auditions. Six office and shop girls with the suitably period names of Cynthia, Maureen, Norah, Elaine, Beryl and Barbara had been chosen from 150 applicants. With the help of 'two days of beauty parlours and hairdressers', these telephonists and typists were now transformed into the archetypal 'Murray's Girl'.[16]

It was no shoo-in. For dancers, experience in tap or ballet was an advantage and many were indeed classically trained. For showgirls, however, the requirements were more lax – that they might be able to follow simple dance steps was enough – though a minimum height of 5ft 7in or thereabouts was often a prerequisite. Becoming a showgirl or hostess was therefore a viable opportunity for those with little previous experience in show business to enter the industry. In 1961, it was estimated that 80 per cent of the girls who were in employment at Murray's were novices in show business. The maximum age for any applicant was usually around 24. An 'attractive personality' was almost always a requirement; so keen was Percival Murray to stress that his showgirls were 'more than a pretty face' that his PR team frequently put out to the press individual showgirl profiles that highlighted their extracurricular interests – and these ran the full gamut of hobbies from tennis to Egyptology!

The perks of employment at Murray's Cabaret Club were enormous: long contracts, free medical services with Harley Street specialists, free manicures,

pedicures, hair appointments and a surprisingly high salary. In 1951, showgirls were earning £6 10s a week. By Keeler's time, this was around £8 a week – almost £2 more than the average woman's wage in those days.

'We want girls who, given the chance, will settle and are keen to progress. We invite the girl's parents to see her in the show as she advances.'[17] Percival Murray set down the rules like a headmaster and even claimed that his club put its girls through a 'charm school' – the only nightclub that 'finds them, feeds them, cossets them, and costumes them.'[18] In reality, this equated to a bevy of attractive new recruits making regular visits to his Surrey estate, where they would all play croquet together and learn how to drop their regional accents for a posher, much-affected 'nightclub accent'. All this in

Percival Murray
welcomes a
group of Murray's
showgirls to
Bookhams, his
country estate.
1961
© British Pathé

order to equip them with an immaculate sense of etiquette so that they might mingle effortlessly with the club's clientele. If Percival Murray's 'grooming' process appears rather dubious, that's because it was. To a select few – those who called him 'Pops' – the relationship was more than paternal. Christine Keeler claims that, though he was a lot older than the girls, 'he had a reputation for running "the best you've ever had" casting couch.'[19] Notably, it was often those girls in his 'inner circle' who were given the principal roles in the floorshows. At least one showgirl went to live with him as a mistress in his Whitehall flat. Another, who was very young when she joined, was made Percival's ward and taken in as his 'adopted daughter'. He regularly whisked them off to the French Riviera, where they would all stay in a luxury hotel, all expenses on Mr Murray. Fancy dinners would be interposed with hard work brainstorming new floorshow themes and scanning the shops for costumes and materials.

Membership

The code of conduct for showgirls was almost as strict as Percival Murray's admissions policy. Only members and their guests were permitted entry. At its prime in the 1950s and early 1960s, there were as many as 92,000 members, but becoming a member meant more than simply paying the annual fee of a guinea. It required vetting – after all, Murray's Cabaret Club was now being billed in *The Stage* as 'London's oldest Luxury Club and the one which has the best and largest Floor Shows in Town'.[20] And such a place needed an equally impressive pedigree of patron. Percival Murray, himself now described as the 'acknowledged elder statesman of the night club world', was looking for statesmen of a more conventional kind as his clientele.[21] Indeed, countless leading politicians numbered amongst his distinguished visitors. One night it might be Henry Kissinger, another night Randolph Churchill, whose father, Winston, was also a customer. Rumour has it that the prime minister would sit behind a screen to maintain his 'discretion'. Royalty might also be present. Prince Philip was a frequent attendee with his Thursday Club friends, as seen recently in the Netflix series, *The Crown*. Princess Margaret and her then-fiancé Billy Wallace came too. Though he would not be the man she married, the Queen's sister needn't have looked so far for the man she in fact did wed: Tony Armstrong-Jones. The young and budding photographer was a regular at the club and even photographed some showgirls in the dressing room for *London*, his first book of photographs, published in 1958.[22] Then there was King Hussein of Jordan, who would bring along a vast contingent of Arab delegates. Amongst this eccentric brew of personalities, haut-monde and demi-monde rubbed shoulders. Tycoons such as Paul Getty mingled with louche 'sales executives' and dubious 'legal professionals' hovering on the fringes of acceptable society. Schlockmeister movie producer and friend of Stephen Ward, Harry Alan Towers, was one such shady figure. He began every evening at Murray's ostensibly writing screenplays for the likes of Orson Welles and Christopher Lee, though was later accused of working out of the club as a Soviet agent. Towers never forgot how Scotland Yard had, with the agreement of Percival Murray, wired certain visitor booths with radio microphones to snoop on supposed spies.

Film stars were omnipresent. The club was a particular favourite with Jean Harlow. Such was the milieu of this high-class establishment that Percival Murray never failed to boast that the 'crowned heads of Europe' sat nightly at his tables.[23] However, Murray never granted admission to openly acknowledged criminals; contrary to popular myth, the Kray twins were never members. 'Tiny little place it is. There was a postage stamp for a dance floor,' recalled the notorious gangster 'Mad' Frankie Fraser. Yet he had to confess that he 'didn't go there a lot because it wasn't really for faces. It was considered a classy brasses' drum for punters.'[24]

Above, left: **Radio and television producer Harry Alan Towers. c.1955**
© Keystone/ Hulton/Getty

Above, right: **The tycoon Paul Getty on a trip to London. 1959**
© Everett/Alamy

Sex

Respectability was always tempered by a risqué undercurrent, and it was this side of Murray's Cabaret Club that Christine Keeler recalled in her autobiography:

> We star showgirls walked bare-breasted on to the stage, and the hostesses, all cleavage and chat, moved among the wealthy and aristocratic middle-aged male diners ... they could look but could not touch. 'Pops' Murray, as he instructed his 'girls' to call him, ran a sort of visual brothel. There was a pervasive atmosphere of sex.[25]

This sensationalist account was no doubt conditioned by the harrowing effect that the Profumo Affair had on Keeler, yet in it there is also more than a kernel of truth.

The only other West End venue that was mounting such extravagant revues in sumptuous, though flimsy, costumes was the Windmill Theatre. Since 1932, the Windmill had developed a renowned variety show which featured nude 'tableaux vivants'. At that time, the Lord Chamberlain had the authority to decide what could be shown on stage. When it came to nudity, he declared that 'if it moves, it's rude'. Since nude statues in museums were permitted, then by extension, topless girls in the Windmill's shows were acceptable, as long as they remained motionless on stage.

But Murray's Cabaret Club was not a theatre. 'Nightclubs,' considered a nightlife columnist in 1964, 'exercise their own brand of fascination which is not always felt in the places open to the public at large.'[26] Whereas the separation of stage and audience at the Windmill reduced its nude shows to a 'safe' spectacle, Murray's was a small club with no such fourth wall. The threat to public morals was supposedly far greater, and rumours persisted of performers making themselves available to clients 'after hours', speculation boosted by the Profumo Affair. Yet the 'brothel'-like atmosphere suggested by Keeler is in fact misleading; Murray's showgirls were generally not 'bare-breasted'. When they *were* topless, the same rules as at the Windmill applied. Adverts for showgirl 'nudes' only ever required applicants to be good at 'posing'[27] –

doing so at the back of the stage behind the (non-nude) dancers, they would form a spectacular visual backdrop. It was only in the tail years of Murray's existence – especially after the abolition of the Lord Chamberlain's powers of censorship in 1968 – that topless performers featured more prominently by dancing at closer quarters to the audience.

Moreover, most of the costume designers at Murray's had worked for the Windmill. They knew the difference between suggestion and overt eroticism. So did Kenneth Bandy, the legendary PR guru for both the Windmill and Murray's, who also took the girls' publicity photographs. A handful of girls, such as Christine Carson and Iris Chapple, performed at both the Windmill and Murray's.

A typical nude tableau vivant at the Windmill Theatre.
1939
© Mander and Mitchenson/ University of Bristol/ArenaPAL

Despite the language in which Christine Keeler couches her description of Murray's, she did admit that the club was 'the only one of its type in London which was not a pick-up place'.[28] 'If anyone "laid a hand" on any of [Percival Murray's] girls they would be thrown out, or if any one of us was discovered "up the lane" after the show with a customer, we would be sacked.'[29]

Though Murray's Cabaret Club was considered a romantic nightspot for couples – even husbands and wives – the customers were overwhelmingly male and the entertainment was clearly for their delectation. Unsurprisingly, therefore, liaisons were not strictly off the agenda away from the nightclub's premises. For example, Murray's dancer and friend of Christine Keeler, Mandy Rice-Davies, met property racketeer and regular customer Peter Rachman at the club. She soon became his mistress. One of Murray's oldest clients, the Earl of Dudley, took such a shine to her that he proposed marriage, and Rice-Davies later claimed that, 'I could have been a dowager duchess by the time I was 22.'[30] 'I wish I had a pound,' said Percival Murray, 'for every one of my girls who has a title.'[31] For working-class girls who dreamed of marrying for money or title, Murray's Cabaret Club was the place this could happen. And it often did.

Alumni

Connections were everything at Murray's Cabaret Club. Although most of the performers inevitably faded into obscurity, a few used the club as a platform from which to launch their careers into show business.

Kay Kendall started out there before becoming a film star. Ruth Ellis was a dancer there before she was convicted of murdering her lover and becoming the last woman to be hanged in the UK in 1955. A little-known fact is that Ruth and Kay knew each other and both starred in Frank Launder and Sidney Gilliat's film *Lady Godiva Rides Again* (1952). Both knew Stephen Ward, who was coming to the club over a decade before the Profumo Affair. One of the first of 'Ward's Girls' was Murray's showgirl Valerie Mewes, the best friend of Ruth Ellis. Ward would transform her into 'Vicki Martin', the hottest glamour model in London, and introduce her to Kay Kendall, with whom she starred in Compton Bennett's 1952 film *It Started in Paradise*. Via Ward's network, she had an affair with the Maharajah of Cooch Behar, a 1950s playboy and horse-racing fanatic. Everyone and everything seemed to be connected. Another associate of this group was the peroxide blonde bombshell Carole Lesley, who sang and danced at the club before becoming a film actress. Sadly, none of these women of the '50s lived beyond their 30s; drugs, alcohol, fast-living and tragic circumstances befell them.

There were many others, now virtually unknown. Tracking them down is not easy, not least because Percival Murray often bestowed upon them exotic stage names. Soubrette Trixie Scales starred in André Charlot's highly

Ruth Ellis, the
year before her
execution.
1954
© *Illustrated
London News/*
Mary Evans
Picture Library

successful musical revues and appeared in many British films, including *In Which We Serve* (1942). She became a friend of John Mills, Frankie Howerd and Edwina Mountbatten, and eventually founded her own theatrical agency. Susan Irvin moved straight from Murray's to landing a leading role in the hit American musical *The Pajama Game* in 1956. Principal dancer Patsy Snell featured in comic period films and television series, including *The Early Bird* (1965) with Norman Wisdom, *Carry On ... Follow that Camel* (1967) and *Up Pompeii* (1971), before marrying comedian Eddie Large. Annette Battam, previously a singer with bandleader Lew Stone, developed a thriving cabaret and musical career. Leading lady Frances Lea was one of the Vernon Girls, and had appeared on film with The Beatles in 1964, before forming one half of singers Fran and Alan. On a more bizarre note, showgirl Mary Ann MacLean became the founder of a satanic cult, The Process Church, in the 1960s, after marrying Robert de Grimston, 'The Christ of Carnaby Street'.

Remarkable happenstance surrounds two particular alumni. Lyse Denise – real name Marie-Lise Volpeliere Pierrot – was a showgirl who became the long-time companion of the actor John Hurt. Her early death while out riding haunted Hurt and has often been credited with moulding his enigmatic persona. It provided him with good reason to revisit her past by starring as Stephen Ward in the film *Scandal* (1989), a fictionalised account of the Profumo Affair. 'Stephen Ward' was also the name of an Andrew Lloyd Webber musical, staged in 2013. Paula Brightman, mother of Lloyd Webber's ex-wife – singer and actress Sarah Brightman – was a contemporary at the club with Christine Keeler. Paula danced there in the early 1960s under the name 'Janey', and this legacy was part inspiration for the musical, many scenes of which take place at a fictionalised Murray's Club with the actor Christopher Howell playing the character of Percival Murray.

Final Act

Murray's Cabaret Club made Percival a very rich man indeed. Aside from Bookhams, the country house he acquired in the early 1940s, he owned sumptuous flats in Whitehall, Mayfair and Bournemouth, a fleet of Rolls Royces and more money than could last a lifetime. But the success didn't last.

In 1966, the Playboy Club opened in London. 'After Bunny-Day,' asked *The Tatler*, 'will London ever be the same again?'[32] The answer would become clear within just a few years, as British society underwent massive changes in the way it regarded sex and women. Murray's Cabaret Club had only ever offered a recipe of mild titillation, but the Playboy Club provided a sleazier cocktail – of sex, drugs and rock 'n' roll. The strip clubs, peep shows and casinos were moving into Soho. This was simply never Percival

John Hurt as
Stephen Ward
with Joanne
Whalley Kilmer as
Christine Keeler
in *Scandal*.
1988
© Moviestore/
Alamy

Murray's scene, even if Murray's Cabaret Club served as the inspiration for the fictional nightclub in *The Long Firm*, the Jake Arnott book and television series that tells the story of Harry Starks's porn empire.[33] Around this time, Percival Murray put his overheads at £4,500 a week, yet limited seating capacity meant the club could accommodate only 120 guests. Percival refused to lower standards by cutting the large staff-to-patron ratio, so David Murray suggested in 1968 that he open a gambling floor. But Percival, something of an old-school purist, refused to 'sacrifice good taste in favour of merely counting the takings', as Peter Hepple put it.[34] David was soon dismissed after a bitter dispute and thrown out penniless onto the street. No-one predicted that he would become successful in the field of biotechnology, as a pioneer in antibody production.

The huge overheads weren't the only problem. In 1959, *The Stage's* Nightbeat columnist, Reg Barlow, discerned the ingredients of Percival Murray's 'foolproof formula' – 'masses of beautiful girls, who sing, dance and parade at close quarters' and 'tip-top speciality acts to entertain at intervals'.[35] But by the mid-1960s the formula was crumbling because tastes were changing. The popularity of recorded music gave birth to the discotheque but, at the same time, killed off the vogue for live dance band music. Murray's Cabaret Club had always championed bandleaders such as Mantovani, Geraldo and Edmundo Ros – almost all forgotten names. Gone were the days when bandleader Al Tabor composed 'The Hokey Cokey' – now a regular fixture at children's birthday parties – at Murray's for the club band in 1940. In 1965, *The Times* reported that those clubs with floorshow entertainments might be tempted to 'drop their floorshows and cabarets and turn themselves into discotheques'.[36]

Rock 'n' roll originated with Britain's youth, but Murray's was never a nightclub for the youth. The young 1950s pop stars Billy Fury and Vince Eager found this out the hard way, when accompanying their manager Larry Parnes to the club; their funds could barely cover the concierge tip, let alone buy the hostesses drinks. Instead of rock 'n' roll, the interval acts who performed at the club tended to be British crooners, variety stars or performers of 'light' pop music. When the singer Dodie West sang there, one reviewer breathed a sigh of relief that, 'despite her fairly recent "mod" image', she instead gave the audience a nice collection of 'folksy numbers, which she puts across with a smiling sincerity'.[37] Singers such as Samantha Jones, Joy Marshall or Dorita y Pepe were just too unfashionable. The irony is that Peter Grant, the club's bouncer on the door, had now left for an enormously successful career in rock music, managing a band called Led Zeppelin. Just as outmoded were the speciality acts. Whereas in the 1950s, demand was high for the magician Gogia Pasha, the mentalist Al Koran, Esme Levante 'The Gorgeous Witch', Noberti, Johnny Lamonte and numerous Chinese plate-spinning acts, such entertainments didn't pass muster in the 1970s.

The writing was on the wall. In a bid to save the club, Percival Murray was driven to bankruptcy and closed up shop in 1975. 'The sad end of an era', declared the *Daily Express*'s 'William Hickey' column.[38] It was saddest for Percival Murray, who spent these years of perpetual ill-health slumped in his palatial bed, amidst a heap of *Playboy* magazines. In 1974, a sprightly young *Daily Mirror* journalist conducted a five-hour interview from the foot of Percival's bed and was unsurprised to learn that 'he still auditions girls and runs the show from the bedroom'. In his monogrammed silk pyjamas and velvet dressing gown, Percival regaled the reporter with tales of Jessie Mathews, Marilyn Monroe and other women he apparently knew and loved. But who was the most beautiful woman he ever loved? 'A difficult question,' Murray replied. 'Jean Harlow I suppose … but then she wasn't a woman. She was a goddess!'[39]

Today, 16–18 Beak Street is a burger bar. Step downstairs to the basement and waitresses, most of whom were born long after the club's closure in 1975, flit between the tables. They serve the tourists of Carnaby Street and Kingly Court. The tiny room has been made even smaller by the expansion of the chef's kitchen. The wood panelling has been whitewashed; it resembles the muddy grey of 'Bombsite Britain' in the 1950s. Post-war, the West End may have been blighted by austerity, but here underground, the oak walls once shimmered as they reflected the sparkle of costumed showgirls dancing. Close your eyes and imagine.

II

TESTIMONY

As time moves on, the people and places of our past slip gradually from sight and sound, only to be reduced to myths and legends. That is, unless they are reliably recorded. Whilst the world of Murray's was obviously very real to those who experienced it, 'experience' is equally ephemeral. It is also deeply personal and, for that reason, difficult to convey.

Nevertheless, the following recollections from three former dancers and showgirls – none of whom knew each other, since they were employed at different times during the club's history – testify to the vitality of Murray's, which remains palpable in their memories. The photographs reproduced throughout the chapter – discovered only recently in the V&A's archives – date to the mid-1960s.

Jean Hendy-
Harris.
c.1962
© Victoria &
Albert Museum

JEAN HENDY-HARRIS (1962–63)

'London was experiencing a new vigour, as if it were aware that the Swinging Sixties was about to begin. Though ordinary people like me were largely unaware of it, we were entering a period of post-War boom. We had more disposable income than our predecessors, so could afford all manner of extravagant household items, such as refrigerators and vacuum cleaners. Even washing machines had, until then, been regarded as luxury items. Whilst the older generation was still preoccupied with ridding itself of the effects of war and deprivation, the young were more and more disinclined to pay heed to their warnings of frugality, and simply threw themselves headlong into a spending frenzy. With the advent of cheap, chain-store clothing lines, fashions changed fast and prices were dropping with equal rapidity. The Twist had arrived, and television had overtaken radio as the most popular form of home entertainment.

In Soho – one of my most beloved areas of the city – the popular music scene was developing at a startling rate. The Marquee Club in Wardour Street, featuring skiffle and blues, had been open since 1958. The Rolling Stones had yet to play their first gig there. Further down the street, La Discotheque – London's original disco, destined to become immensely popular – was about to open. Nearby, El Condor, owned by Peter Rachman, was already being managed by the infamous criminal, Raymond Nash. The Bag O'Nails in Kingly Street had been doing a roaring trade for several years. A vast array of unregistered drinking clubs had also sprung up in Soho, very possibly as a result of the 1959 Street Offences Act that had effectively cleared the streets of prostitutes. They morphed into club hostesses or were giving French lessons on the upper floors of the old buildings. The area continued to harbour all the necessary ingredients for the various elements of vice, and was synonymous with sex and general depravity.

Murray's Cabaret Club, situated in a Beak Street basement, was one of Soho's most renowned nightspots at this time. Percy Murray, who liked his staff to call him 'Pops', was a strange man who never failed to remind me of a department store Santa Claus. The club was famous for its lavish floorshows, where dozens of showgirls paraded the small stage in glamorous and exotic costumes.

On my frequent ramblings in the area, safely in daylight hours, I had always stopped to examine the posters and photographs outside, allowing myself to be envious of the girls who worked there. One day, I noticed a small handwritten sign: 'Showgirls Wanted – No Experience Needed'. Surely that couldn't be correct. A showgirl unquestionably had to know what she was doing. She would have to know how to dance, for one thing. The hated quickstep flashed in front of me and I shuddered. I was a shorthand typist – not a showgirl. But then it *did* say in the most unambiguous terms that no experience was necessary.

That evening, I diligently practised the Twist in preparation. The next afternoon I bought a very expensive low-cut bra and matching satin briefs from the lingerie department at Whiteleys and set off for the West End, wearing the satin underclothes and a great deal of make-up.

'Mr Murray is auditioning this Friday,' the short-sighted receptionist said, in a tone of complete disinterest. 'Come back then. 3 p.m.'

When I did, I found myself joined in the lobby by half a dozen other hopefuls. We were directed one-by-one into Mr Murray's office, where he sat behind his vast desk, looking more than ever like an affable Father Christmas. He leaned towards me and shook my hand awkwardly as he asked my name, which I changed immediately on the spot to Jane.

'Well nice to meet you, Jane. Ever done any work like this before?'

'No,' I told him as brightly as possible, adding as an afterthought a dazzling smile. 'Not at all.'

He wanted to ascertain, first of all, whether I could 'move to music', telling me that there was nothing to dancing; it was all a question of whether you had a feel for rhythm or not. I swayed about the room to some tune I no longer remember, before he asked me to remove my sweater and skirt to have a look at my body. I held my stomach in as resolutely as possible. 'Very good legs,' he said, more to himself than to me. '*Very* good legs.'

And a couple of minutes later I was hired.

'You get £9 a week, dear,' he said, making notes on a piece of paper in front of him.

One of the head showgirls was detailed to show me and two other successful girls the ropes. We had to turn up to rehearsals. We had to keep the costumes we were allocated in good repair. We were not allowed to fraternise too closely with the clientele.

'What do you actually mean?' asked a girl called Marie.

'No case jobs,' the head showgirl answered.

I soon discovered the term meant we were not allowed to sleep with clients for money. I was extremely relieved because I had no intention of doing so. In fact, the thought had never crossed my mind. I was there to be a glamorous showgirl, and believed that once I had the various dance routines under my belt, I would quit Murray's for traditional variety theatre via dance troupes such as The Bluebells or The Tillers. I pictured a very direct route to the top – very possibly, and not before too long, with my name in lights outside at least one West End theatre. I had yearned for this since the age of 16.

Emerging daily from the Tube station and catching glimpses of myself in Regent Street windows, I was reassured that at least I looked the part. Although the other girls grumbled when rehearsals went over time, I was simply delighted to be part of the production and happy to stay hour after hour executing dance steps. Fortunately for me, the form of dancing required by a showgirl came almost naturally. Two weeks from the first rehearsal I was thrust with little ceremony into the middle of the back row of dancers. A week

later, I was appointed understudy to Geraldine, a front row girl with a much more prominent position. I was almost delirious with delight; all thoughts of shorthand and typing rapidly evaporated.

There were two cabarets each evening. Between shows, we were expected to sit out with the customers and could earn as much as £5 in hostess fees each time. The girls who were married or engaged could opt out of hostess obligations but Pops tried not to employ too many who fell into that category. I quickly found that he had a habit of developing short-lived crushes on some of his employees and I tried hard not to do anything that caused him to notice me too much. This proved more and more difficult as the weeks passed because Pops was decidedly a 'legs man'.

The clientele all appeared completely ancient with the exception of a group of wealthy young Arabs who were supposed to be studying at the London School of Economics. Our hostess duties gave us the choice of ordering fruit cups at 18s each or champagne at £7 a bottle. I learned that the fruit cups were the best bet if I were to perform the second floorshow with any degree of precision.

The club customers were by no means all male, although that was generally the case from Monday to Thursday. Fridays and Saturdays were called 'Family Nights' by Pops, who staunchly claimed that he ran a family-oriented business in spite of our near nakedness. The Monday-to-Thursday regulars rarely brought in their wives and mothers, but that was most definitely not the case later in the week.

Although Murray's Cabaret Club has earned a somewhat notorious reputation in the years since it closed, it was actually, for the most part, a well-thought-of establishment and its regular customers included people like Princess Margaret, King Hussein and various Peers of the Realm, as well as the great and the good amongst the business fraternity.

One night, I sat with a club regular, Stephen, who was only in his late 40s but at the time seemed like an old man. He could easily be spared the senior citizen category on account of his extraordinary charm and charisma. 'You were sensational in the cabaret,' he told me, and went on to demand that I tell him all about myself. He listened attentively, eyes always on my face and urging me to tell him more. Handing me two £5 notes, he asked for my

telephone number, which I gave him at once. At that point, the band struck up 'The Lady is a Tramp', which was our signal to leave the tables and get ready for the second performance of the evening. But Stephen had left an impression on me. It was well-known that showgirls from Murray's would stay in his Wimpole Mews flat, availing themselves of his hospitality, and I had seen him regularly in the club, often quite alone. I asked one of the other girls if she knew anything about him.

'He doesn't usually pay to go case,' she said, 'but he's quite generous with hostess fees and will sometimes pay you to go to a party with him – if he can't persuade you for nothing, that is.'

And that is precisely what happened. Within a short space of time, he had asked me to accompany him to a dinner party to be given by friends of his who had a house in Hyde Park Square, offering me money when I seemed less than keen.

'You may find them slightly eccentric, darling. Hod is an antiques dealer and his wife is Czech. She's terribly sexy. They provide the most fabulous food, really exotic dishes. At the really big parties there has been roast peacock. They always have fascinating guests. All kinds of people: government officials, surgeons, lawyers and even once a bishop.'

He took me shopping to buy a suitable dress from Harrods, which was designed to make me look every inch a high-class tart struggling to become an acceptable society lady. I later came to know these friends of his – Horace Dibben and his striking wife Mariella Novotny – very well. Mariella had left home in her teens to become a striptease dancer and part-time prostitute. She had worked in Washington and enjoyed relationships with leading politicians, including both Jack and Bobby Kennedy. A boyfriend – television producer and Murray's regular, Harry Alan Towers – had lured her to the United States. She had only gone because she had wanted to become famous and do something to make her widowed mother proud. The trip, however, resulted in both she and Towers being charged with violation of the White Slave Trafficking Act, with Mariella also informing the FBI that Towers was acting as a Soviet agent. She returned to Britain in 1961 and now turned her hand to running sex parties in London for the amusement and edification of her husband and his friends.

Stephen took me to these parties, where we would drink excellent champagne before dinners of caviar, stilton cheese, and roast venison with red cabbage. We usually sat around a large table that had a huge ice-sculpted penis as a centrepiece. Mariella would then appear, whip in hand, so that the attendees, including myself, could act out all sorts of sexual fantasies. Generally speaking, the guests were the same sorts of people – lawyers, doctors, mathematicians and civil servants. Into these groups of outwardly staid and ordinary married couples, Stephen injected a succession of well-paid and pretty young girls selected from Murray's Cabaret Club. After another hour or so, we would all gather in the elegant drawing room, drinking more coffee, the men discussing stock prices, the women talking of babysitters and school fees.

As the months went by, I got to know the (later much reviled) Stephen Ward a great deal better. Those parties would become a regular occurrence, beginning with drinks and genteel conversation, often about the latest gossip on Pops Murray and his girls, followed by a dinner of grouse, pheasant or hare. After dinner, we would get down to the main business of the evening: sado-masochistic sex.

Although I was initially enthralled by the glamour of working as a show-girl, the allure wore off remarkably quickly and I began to get more and more irritated by the surfeit of petty rules imposed upon us by Pops. Every now and again he would order a shoe inspection and if our shoes, which we had to provide ourselves, did not blend with our costumes to his satisfaction, he would impose fines left, right and centre. He would also, unannounced, inspect our hair to ensure it was correctly styled; if not, then the same fines came firing from his office. It seemed to depend entirely upon his mood. So I decided to leave Murray's for the more relaxed atmosphere of the Jack of Club's nightclub on Brewer Street. When I told my colleagues there that I had worked at Murray's, they were immediately impressed. Little did I realise that I had left just before the Profumo Affair broke, a saga that revolved around Jack Profumo, who had a reputation for bullying and threatening so many of the women I knew back at Murray's.

I went on to work in many other clubs, including L'Hirondelle on Swallow Street and Danny La Rue's club in Hanover Square, where Judy Garland and her daughter could always be relied on to join in the cabaret at the drop of a hat. But of all the clubs I worked during those years, Murray's was certainly the most exciting and undoubtedly the most glamorous.

**Iris Chapple.
Late 1950s**
© Iris Chapple/
Edgar Brind

IRIS CHAPPLE (1963–73)

'A singer?! You'll never do anything with your life as a singer. You will never get anywhere,' the headteacher shouted. It was 1952 and I didn't care. I left school to sing in a Latin American dive in Soho, opposite a coffee shop where I used to see the infamous Iron Foot Jack. It led to a job soon afterwards singing jazz in the Ballerina Club, Gerrard Street, with a well-known black pianist called Cab Kaye. 'Shakey' Sheila ran the place, which was no more than a sleazy clip joint next to the studios of Harrison Marks, the softcore photographer, who was holed up there with his muse, Pamela Green. The area was not yet Chinatown. For now, it was all Italians. The Messina Brothers ran their protection rackets on these streets. I didn't like working there; the men were aggressive and you never knew whether they'd have a knife or gun in hand when they asked you to come home with them. I never obliged: I was an entertainer, there to perform for people, not some call girl.

This was the early '50s. There weren't many clubs around at the time so you'd see the same characters in the same dives around Soho. I remember Peter Rachman – the slum landlord who was buying up Notting Hill at the time. This was long before he was with Mandy Rice-Davies. He used to go around the bars with a blonde gunrunner. I used to see Kay Kendall – a former Murray's girl – too. She was a friend of Diana Dors, who was *always* down the clubs with her husband Dennis. They knew Ruth Ellis, who was at Murray's a few years before myself, and had an equally dubious reputation; I was always hearing of their drug-fuelled orgies at their home in Maidenhead.

Dean Street, Frith Street, Greek Street, Beak Street – there wasn't a road in Soho that we walked along where we didn't meet at least five people whom we knew. I remember Francis Bacon. He tried to flog me one of his paintings.

'Look, Iris, I will give you three pictures for twenty quid,' he said.

'I don't want them.'

'Why not? It's three for £20!'

'Because I don't *like* them, Francis.'

And to think I could have actually bought them back then! This isn't to say I was no bohemian. In fact, these were the last days of Bohemian Soho, where

I would walk down Old Compton Street with my friend, the film director John Paddy Carstairs, wearing wooden earrings, black cut-off tights, eyes jet black, and with no shoes on!

In 1953, I went on tour with Cy Laurie. Again, this was pre-rock 'n' roll, pre-skiffle even. We were still firmly in the jazz age. Don Arden, Sharon Osbourne's dad, was a singer on this tour and I remember telling him that when I returned to London, I would try to join the famous Windmill Theatre, which I did in 1957. It was good fun and I got to mix with the likes of Mickie Most, Engelbert Humperdinck and Tom Jones.

Around this time, I was taken on by Harold Miller, a vocal coach who taught virtually *everybody* in the business. Me and Helen Shapiro were already having lessons with Freddie Winrose in Denmark Street, but Harold was really brilliant. He was coaching Shirley Bassey at the time. 'Listen to Iris,' he would tell Shirley. 'She *sings*. You *shout*.' Then Sean Connery would come in for elocution lessons with Harold's wife – anything to rid himself of his strong Scottish accent now he was becoming a serious actor.

Eventually, I was scouted by Paul Raymond, for whom I worked in 1962, performing at the Raymond Revuebar in Walker's Court and the Celebrite Club on Clifford Street. At the time, he was constantly being chased by the authorities on obscenity charges and when he tried to get me to take off my bra, I reminded him that he had hired me as a singer, and promptly left.

I did a stint at L'Hirondelle, followed by the Stork, which was run by my agent's father, the impresario Al Burnett. But I wasn't used to mixing with the rough types who went there, even if they spent lots of money and Princess Margaret came. The Krays used to be in there all the time in 1962. The head waiter always warned me if they were in the room, so I could leave through the back door after my shift; if I went through the front door, they'd pester me to have a drink at their table. A lot of girls didn't decline such invitations; I remember seeing Christine Keeler at their table more than once.

Murray's Cabaret Club was a totally different environment. The Kray twins would not have been tolerated on the pavement outside the club, let alone inside. This was serious show business. Whilst the Windmill Theatre had great cachet, it was not the place for women to launch a career in show business. It was a repertory theatre which felt like an extension of stage school. Few of my friends at the Windmill had actually advanced onto the West End stage; most ended up performing there for a short period before becoming wholesome housewives with children. Murray's was just not that sort of environment – it was an extremely exclusive and upmarket private members' club for the rich and famous, many of whom we got to know intimately.

I joined Murray's in 1963 and soon realised that a handful of girls from the Windmill had also joined, like Denise Warren, Christine Carson and Polly Perkins, who rose to fame as a teen pop star before becoming a staple of television soap operas, including *EastEnders*. My good friend Perin Lewis also left the Windmill for Murray's. She too knew Diana Dors, and was actually married to that rock 'n' roll singer Vince Taylor, who turned out to be David Bowie's hero.

Throughout 1963, I remember being pestered nightly by journalists, week-on-week, asking for Christine and Mandy. It was right at the time of the Profumo Affair and, whilst the main protagonists were no longer coming to the club, Lord Astor was just about still coming. I do recall meeting Ivanov, but made little of him. He was just one of many Russian attachés visiting each night.

The first thing that struck me on joining Murray's was how sophisticated the girls were. They had to be; the old man, Mr Murray, would never have had a dumb blonde working for him, because we needed to be capable of conversation with the high-class customers. So the girls came into work dressed impeccably. I would wear all sorts of fashionable suedes and silks by Norman Hartnell, Jean Muir, Bill Gibb and Jean Varon. Every girl seemed to have a sable coat and diamond rings. It was nothing like the tacky fag-smoking atmosphere, depicted in the film *Scandal*, of girls sitting around in their bikinis.

The job never felt exploitative – only empowering. You were never obliged to join someone as a hostess if you didn't want to. A few of the girls ended up marrying customers, some of them even gaining titles. Personally, I enjoyed hostessing when I was not singing, especially because the old man Mr Murray would put an extra £5 on the bill for you. This is how I came to know Paul Getty, though he was a miserable old bugger – he was unbelievably mean when it came to the bill; I can't remember him ever paying. Then there was Lord Lucan, Peter Shand Kydd, David Frost and Sidney Poitier, whose gorgeous wife caused all the showgirls' jaws to drop when she walked into the place wearing an extravagant full-length white mink coat.

A few especial clients I got to know particularly well. British Ambassador Sir Horace Phillips became a good friend. The King of Nepal also liked to request my company for a drink. So well did I get to know the President of Liberia, William Tolbert, that he would invite me to his house. This was only a few years before his assassination. The High Commissioner to India actually flew me out to Delhi, and put me (and my friends!) up in an expensive hotel, just to sing at an event there. The Chief Minister of Malaysia once took me and another Murray's girl to lunch at the Ritz. Afterwards, he allowed me to drive his very beautiful, very large Mercedes. As we drove up Park Lane, the police stopped the traffic to let us through, and others were saluting us along the road. Only when we got to Marble Arch did we realise that the flag on the front of the car was not the Malaysian one but the British Royal Arms; but for the flag, the royal car was identical to the minister's Mercedes so the Ritz's valet had mixed them up! We remained lifelong friends after I left Murray's. He even picked up my mum from her house in Brixton to take her to the Cabaret Club to watch my show. She ended up drinking so much champagne that she was sick and sent home!

It was as though Mr Murray had brought the Folies Bergère from Paris to London. Those costumes: real furs, real silks, semi-precious stones ... not even the Windmill Theatre, whose girls wore beautiful costumes, could afford to spend the money that Mr Murray did in this respect. The Eve Club costumes were nowhere near as upmarket either. This is what made Murray's Cabaret Club totally unique.

It was the old man's pride to get the girls in his private room downstairs where he would fit them, occasionally – though not too often – with Mrs Burchmore. He would test me by suggesting slits in all sorts of revealing places, but I would always laugh it off and refuse to bare too much. No doubt, other girls – especially those who were 16 or 17, rather than in their '20s – played along. He liked to have an army of young girls around him, some of whom even lived with him, though I declined his invitations to go to the

South of France with him. Those girls who did go seemed to enjoy being chauffeured around in his open-top Rolls Royce and being showered with the beautiful clothes he bought for them. Many girls expressed how Mr Murray had nurtured them in an environment less vulnerable than their chaotic lives back home. Personally, I loved going to his beautiful flat in Whitehall Court, where us singers would do our rehearsals.

In the late '60s, I started getting into transcendental meditation. I went to stay with an inspirational guru on an ashram in the Himalayas, not far from Rishikesh, where The Beatles were practising the art. I was still singing at Murray's whenever I came back to London, but the old man was getting exasperated at my teetotalism and vegetarianism. How was I going to drink champagne and eat lobster with the clients now?! I was the only member of the company allowed to stick with fruit cups, and cauliflower cheese or mushrooms on toast. What's more, my guru felt I should stop singing in nightclubs. So I eventually left Murray's to become a television presenter at the BBC and, subsequently, an actress in *Kismet* when it went on tour.

Memories of those days are often triggered. Just the other day I was reading about John Hurt's girlfriend; she died in a freak accident which led Hurt, who was grief-stricken, to take on the leading role in *Scandal*. At the time I didn't know any of this because she went under the stage name of Lyse Denise. She was a lovely girl. In fact, I only learned about so many of my colleagues later in life. In recent times, I have been a celebrity manicurist and remember one day doing nails for the model Naomi Campbell. We soon established that her mother was in fact the coffee girl who worked at Murray's when I was there. I was able to recall her as she was the only black girl Mr Murray employed.

Murray's put me in the public eye in so many interesting ways. Ken Bandy, our PR guy, was adamant that we did as many adverts as we could, and, after I joined Murray's, I had so many bit parts in various television series from *Z-Cars* to *Danger Man*. Whenever I am watching the old movies from the '60s on television, I can't help but feel how familiar they are, before spotting myself in them! To know I was part of some 'scene' is something so magical.

Murray's Cabaret Club

Murray's Cabaret Club

Teena Symonds: showgirls were not allowed to take photographs behind-the-scenes, but this one was taken on a camera smuggled into the dressing rooms. *c.*1974
© Teena Symonds

TEENA SYMONDS (1973–74)

'Our entrance was through a fairly small door and up the stairs to the performers' dressing room. This was a huge space adorned with counter-style dressing tables. On one side were the dancers, on the other were the showgirls. The singers were at the end. Guarding the door was Mrs Syder – though we called her 'Spud' – an elderly, fairly immobile matron of a lady, who always clucked over us, tutting like a mother hen. She was our guardian, and no man came near our changing room while she was there. The atmosphere was convent-like. Each girl had to sign in with Spud by 9.30 p.m., before the first show began. She always seemed to be repairing our white flannelette G-strings.

Downstairs, individual dressing rooms, which reminded me of small railway carriages, ran the length of a backstage corridor, each an Aladdin's cave housing its own set of gorgeous costumes. These were used by the dancers for quick changes; stripping off their current costume, they would have to hang it up with all its accessories, carefully but swiftly, before hurrying into the next room to slip on the next costume. Tights were disallowed because they would have snagged on the heavily-beaded garments. Jewellery was also a challenge; there was simply not enough time to change earrings or necklaces, so these were attached to our headdresses, which themselves were often so high that we had to duck to exit the dressing-room door. All these costumes were made on the old man's country estate.

The stage area was a very small space considering the number of dancers and showgirls who adorned it. Crimson lampshades sat on small tables, around which were placed velvet chairs. It gave the place a feeling of warmth and decadence. Somewhere, in small cubicles around the stage, were the band; we never saw them apart from occasionally catching sight of one of the musicians squeezing into their confined space or the flicker of the conductor's baton!

I was a Head Girl. There were two of us and we would work out who would perform each part. We also had our very own numbers, specifically choreographed for us. The nine principal dancers and singers were 'swings'; that is, they covered multiple parts and performed any that needed to be covered on any particular night. This meant that they had to know all the positions of each of the forty company performers. Some, like me, were trained at the top performing arts schools. Most of the performers were showgirls – not trained dancers – dressed in feathers and furbelows, which added to the glamour. Four were topless, bare-breasted, not unlike the Bluebell Girls in Paris, though it was all very tasteful. Because of the huge number of girls involved – not all were totally reliable – each show was guaranteed to be different, exciting and sometimes plain scary! Each number/song lasted little more than two minutes. Each had a different singer and set of backing dancers. Each had its own costumes and set. The medley of numbers ran in continuous succession, so the show had to be fast-moving and varied.

Sadly, I lost touch with my fellow dancers. I didn't even know their real names; Mr Murray bestowed stage names on so many of his girls, so Barbaras and Doreens and Joans became Mitzis and Toinettes (yes, they did!) and Candys. I managed to keep my own name as it was a little unusual – 'Teena' with two 'e's. We never used surnames.

Mr Murray looked after his girls. He made sure that those coming from distant counties had excellent accommodation. As Head Girl, I was awarded a flat in St Martin's Lane, as I often had to rehearse new girls. I didn't use it all the time; home was in Windsor, where I would put my children to bed before driving into London to do the shows, only returning home at 3 a.m.

Murray's was not cheap; it was for classy nights out – very special occasions. The customers were wealthy, and businessmen would bring in clients whom they wished to impress. Each night there would be some politician or member of the aristocracy amongst the audience.

If a party of businessmen came in and wanted some female conversation and glamour, hostesses were available to join them. Doreen Dale, the manageress, made sure there was no unpleasantness. Sometimes, clients asked for specific dancers to join the group, and if she were agreeable she could join them, but was under no pressure to do so; the customer would just be told they were unavailable. There was a strict rule that we were only ever allowed to drink champagne; it was good both for the club and us girls, as we rarely had time for more than a glass and no one could mix our drinks. On the odd night that I joined customers, I found that hostessing could be very entertaining. In fact, I married one particular customer, who came frequently to our show and had asked to meet me. We now have six grown-up children.

Murray's launched my show business career. Since those days, I have danced at the London Palladium, starred in a Ken Russell movie, acted in television programmes, taught choreography, chaperoned at Glyndebourne Opera, and opened my very own stage school to train a new generation of talent.

Testimony

69

Murray's
Cabaret Club
BEAK ST. REGENT ST. LONDON W.I

III

SURVIVAL

'There's nothing much left of it in Soho except the legend and the memories'

Christine Keeler

The programme brochures were of deluxe quality. This one recently sold online for £52. c.1963. © Rachel Levy/ Benjamin Levy

For years, it seemed that Christine Keeler was right; all physical traces of Murray's Cabaret Club were apparently scattered to the winds, the whiff of exotica extinguished. After the club went under in 1975, only the original signage for the staff entrance was salvaged for safekeeping. It is now in the possession of Shaftesbury PLC, the property investment company that manages most of Soho. However, in recent years, some items have begun to surface: menus, brochures, matchbooks and other ephemera, such as the lampshades that once graced the nightclub's tables, are regularly sold on eBay, Etsy and other online auction sites. 'Two great pieces of history and very rare' was the seller's description of a pair of rudimentary flower stands that were sold online for as much as £50 in 2018.

As for the costumes, they were bought in 1975 by Elsie Burchmore – Percival Murray's longstanding wardrobe mistress – from the club's liquidators. Percival Murray, now bankrupt, no longer had the funds to acquire them. He had been relegated to living out his last days in what was once the chauffeur's lodge on his estate in Churt, Surrey. Elsie sold off the bulk of the collection – 300 costumes – in 1984, in an auction in nearby Godalming. Sadly, these costumes have now also been widely dispersed; their tatty G-strings, bras, headdresses and jewel cuffs frequently appear on eBay, often available to buy at very little expense. On the other hand, after successful bidding on a handful of costumes, the Victoria & Albert Museum – the premier institution for objects related to theatre and performance – treats them, by comparison, as tantamount to holy relics. They nest in padded storage boxes behind numerous alarmed doors in one of London's most secure museum safehouses.

Photographs and Film Footage

It is difficult for those who did not visit Murray's at the time to get much sense of the club's interiors or its showgirls' costumes, let alone the atmosphere of the floorshows. It is a frustrating truth that Percival Murray banned the performers and customers from taking photographs, and rarely allowed film cameras on the premises.

However, hundreds of publicity photos – previously undisturbed, uncatalogued and undated – have recently come to light in the V&A's Theatre & Performance Archives (see the photographs reproduced throughout the previous chapter). Most are headshots of the showgirls and hostesses in costume, but there are just as many of the cigarette girls, the coat-check girls, the waiters, the musicians, the barmen, the choreographers and Percival Murray himself. Interior shots give a helpful impression of the venue's intimacy.

It is possible to date these to the mid-1960s, from the showgirls and floorshows photographed. Many are of 'Les Femmes du Monde', a floorshow first staged in 1965, in which the girls represented various nationalities, 'graphically illustrating feminine pulchritude from England to

This Michael Bronze costume is handmade from silver lamé fabric, lined with turquoise cotton, and edged with large diamantes set in pink velvet. Though the sleeves are well-worn with frayed feathers and discoloured baubles, it would have once sparkled spectacularly on the dance floor. It sold on eBay in 2018. Late 1950s/ early 1960s © Rachel Levy/ Charlie Jeffreys

A heavily-beaded headdress in the V&A's collection with interlinked chain of silver balls and embellished wristband. It is made of blue paste gems, silver diamantes, silk and feathers. The photograph shows the headdress as it appeared in the floorshow 'Les Femmes du Monde'.
c.1965
© Victoria & Albert Museum

Latin America', in the words of Peter Hepple, the journalist who tirelessly championed the club.[40] Though the costumes are extravagant and obviously very costly, few are themed or display the same ingenuity as those from the halcyon days of Ronald Cobb and Michael Bronze in the 1950s and early 1960s. Many resemble standard showgirl costumes, and the appearance of topless dancers amongst the photographs suggests that some were taken in the club's final years.

There is also some remarkable footage in *Cabaret Girl*, a 26-minute documentary, directed by Guy Blanchard, in the British Film Institute's archives. This gloriously kitsch film in gaudy Technicolor, produced with high

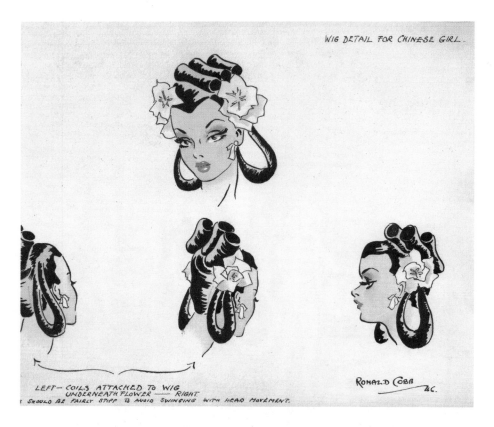

WIG DETAIL FOR CHINESE GIRL.

LEFT — COILS ATTACHED TO WIG
UNDERNEATH FLOWER —— RIGHT.
SHOULD BE FAIRLY STIFF TO AVOID SWINGING WITH HEAD MOVEMENT.

RONALD COBB 46.

Ronald Cobb's suggested hairstyle for the 1946 'Limehouse Blues' number. The wig designs on p.75 are Michael Bronze's for the 1956 'Enchantment' number'.
© Mary Evans Picture Library

production values, was made in 1956. It presents a fly-on-the-wall account of the entire process by which a floorshow at Murray's Cabaret Club was conceived and mounted. As Percival and David Murray are shown auditioning the aspiring showgirls, the commentator, in one of many dated quips, remarks that, 'These are the faces that make a company director forget how bored he is in the boardroom.' Smoking endless cigarettes throughout, Percival Murray is shown lecturing his girls on the trials and travails of show business, inspecting their costumes and conducting meetings with the choreographer and lyricist Laurel Grey, the bandleader Harry Lawrence, and Michael Bronze, who can be seen preparing the costume designs in his studio.

There is an undeniably prurient aspect to the film, with showgirls adopting provocative poses, stripping off for massages and tanning topless under

FRONT

(A)

(B)

(C)

BACK

1 OF THIS

1 OF THIS

1 OF THIS

1 Michael BRONZE 56

3 OF THESE

FRONT

6 OF THESE

FRONT

1 OF THIS

FRONT

G
H
I
J
K
L

(M)

BACK

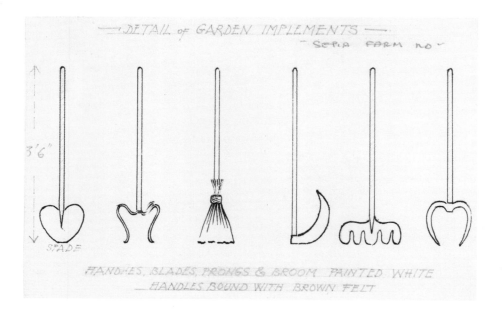

Ronald Cobb's
sketch for a
range of garden
implements that
served as props in
the 'Sepia Farm'
number.
1951
© Mary Evans
Picture Library

Percival Murray
discussing Ronald
Cobb's costume
designs with Elsie
Burchmore.
1961
© British Pathé

a sunlamp. An audience, consisting mostly of couples of mismatched ages, watch a floorshow, the older men twiddling their moustaches, and the younger women in glamorous evening dresses sipping champagne.

Further reels of silent film footage taken by Pathé from as early as 1933 show the various floorshows. They also shed light on Percival Murray's so-called charm school: a legion of showgirls descends upon his Surrey estate and, with more than a little voyeurism, are filmed giggling on sun loungers and playing croquet in the grounds. Meanwhile, Percival Murray and Elsie Burchmore sit in the garden sifting through and discussing two albums' worth of costume designs.

The Costume Designs

In 2014, over fifty years after this footage was recorded, those very same albums of costume designs came to light in Surrey. The family of Elsie Burchmore auctioned these as the last vestiges of the collection she had acquired from the club's liquidators. Hidden away for decades, this treasure trove was spotted by vintage poster dealer Charlie Jeffreys, who bought the portfolio of costume designs when he visited the auction on a whim. They are arguably the most important surviving physical artefacts from Murray's Cabaret Club, and, never before published in their entirety, form the core of this catalogue.

Their ingenuity and inventive wit is striking. The sketched mannequins – often surprised-looking girls – revel in their status as saucy pin-ups. Their costumes are revealing; some are no more than a headdress and G-string, the two defining components of the cabaret showgirl's costume. Though many drawings feature bare breasts, Elsie Burchmore's seamstresses usually ensured – at least until the club's final decade – that breasts were covered when the costumes were eventually tailored. Murray's Cabaret Club was, categorically, never a strip club.

Rather than conforming to the 'conventional' showgirl costume of feathered headdress and suspenders with netted tights, these sophisticated designs do

A showgirl models
Michael Bronze's
costume for
the 'Witchcraft'
number in
Percival Murray's
home.
1961
© British Pathé

what the best cabaret costumes do: they adopt thematic elements similar to costumes worn in British pantomime. That is, they frequently incorporate references and symbols that illustrate the particular theme of the floorshow for which they were designed – anything from varieties of perfume to fairy tales.

The designs notably provide a considerable amount of detail. Often this includes the name of the floorshow, the specific number within that floorshow, the name of the particular dancer who is to wear the costume, her role in the show, her position on stage and the name of the accompanying piece of music. Others are simply illustrations for suggested hairstyles, wigs, props or menu designs (p.104). Each costume was fitted individually, often with as many as ten fittings before the dress was passed as satisfactory. Some sketches provide precise measurements and copious instructions as to which materials to use, and the necessary colours; in a few cases, fabric samples have been pasted onto the designs survive. Such details were immensely important to Percival Murray, who took great care over his selection of costume designs.

Once Percival Murray had made a decision, the designs passed on to Elsie Burchmore and her team of six seamstresses, who worked all year round in permanent employment from a workshop on Mr Murray's estate in the country. 300 hours was the average time spent on each costume, because of the extremely elaborate jewelling and ornamentation, every single component intricately stitched by hand. Many used thousands of tiny beads or sparkling sequins. The expense of the fabrics matched the level of craftsmanship; for example, only real furs and real silks were used. Once the costumes were created, the girls would model them for Percival Murray and Elsie Burchmore on a replica of the club's stage specially built in his mansion, so that they might judge exactly what each dress would look like in the club. At this stage, many further modifications to the garment might be made.

After they were worn for a show, the costumes returned to the seamstresses, who worked tirelessly on restitching them to ensure that they were good as new for the next performance. Every floorshow comprised three numbers, each requiring approximately forty costumes and, in 1961, estimated to represent a total outlay of £10,000 in materials and labour – that is, £30,000 for one show (over half a million pounds in today's terms) – making the Murray's Cabaret Club girls the most expensively clothed showgirls in town.

A selection of the costume designs was exhibited for the first time in 2018, in Soho. The occasion aroused not only much interest in Murray's Cabaret Club, but also showcased the significant talents of the designers: Ronald Cobb and Michael Bronze, amongst others. All were once well-known names on the nightclub circuit, yet history has not been kind to any of them. In a world where fashion designers and costumiers for film and theatre tend to get the glory of recognition, this catalogue reveals the endlessly creative imaginations of those underrated costume designers who chose Murray's Cabaret Club as their stage.

Soundtrack

What did Murray's *sound* like? Below is a suggested playlist inspired by the type of music that would have been heard during the club's heyday from the early 1950s through to the mid-1960s: cabaret sirens (Eartha Kitt, Shirley Bassey), singers of 'light' music (Alma Cogan), British crooners (Frankie Vaughan), movie stars (Diana Dors), variety stars (Max Bygraves), bandleaders (Mantovani, Geraldo), rockers (Cliff Richard), swooners (Dickie Valentine), honky-tonk novelties (Russ Conway), Bohemian warblers (George Melly), dulcet tones (Matt Monroe), smoky jazz (Johnny Dankworth), Lionel Bart numbers from the period's films and musicals … even Mandy Rice-Davies. Amongst these sixty songs, the hits mingle with the obscurities, the obvious with the eclectic:

The Andrews Sisters – 'Sabre Dance' (1948)
Edmundo Ros – 'The Fidgety Samba' (1951)
Eartha Kitt – 'Let's Do It (Let's Fall in Love)' (1951)
Lita Roza – 'Blacksmith Blues' (1952)
Guy Mitchell – 'She Wears Red Feathers' (1952)
Stargazers – 'Broken Wings' (1953)
Geraldo – 'Prelude to Peace' (1953)
Mantovani – 'The Moulin Rouge Theme' (1953)
Ray Anthony – 'The Hokey Pokey' (1953)
Perry Como – 'Papa Loves Mambo' (1954)
Shake Keane – 'Mambo Indio' (1954)
Johnny Dankworth – 'Perdido' (1954)
Perez Prado – 'Skokiaan' (1954)
Alma Cogan – 'Mambo Italiano' (1955)
Dean Martin – 'Memories Are Made Of This' (1955)
Frankie Laine – 'The Gandy Dancer's Ball' (1955)
Frances Day – 'Heartbreak Hotel' (1956)
Humphrey Lyttelton – 'Bad Penny Blues' (1956)
Winifred Atwell – 'The Poor People of Paris' (1956)
Stanley Black – 'Os Quindins de Yaya' (1957)
Frankie Vaughan – 'The Garden of Eden' (1957)
Shirley Bassey – 'Sex' (1957)
Michael Holliday – 'The Story of My Life' (1958)

Jack Parnell – 'Kick Off' (1958)

Lord Rockingham's XI – 'Hoots Mon!' (1958)

Maxine Daniels – 'Lola's Heart' (1958)

George Melly – 'After You've Gone' (1959)

Vivian Ellis – 'Saturday: Wasp in the Jam' (1959)

Cliff Richard – 'Living Doll' (1959)

Russ Conway – 'Side Saddle' (1959)

Lucille Mapp – 'Chinchilla' (1959)

Dickie Valentine – 'Venus' (1959)

Sheila Buxton – 'Shakedown' (1959)

Anne Heywood – 'Love Is' (1959)

Valerie Masters – 'Say When' (1959)

Eve Boswell – 'Wimoweh Cha Cha' (1959)

Sylvia Sands – 'Love Me Now! Love Me Now! Love Me Now!' (1959)

Brian Hyland – 'Itsy Bitsy Teeny Weeny Yellow Polkadot Bikini' (1960)

Max Bygraves – 'Fings Ain't Wot They Used T'Be' (1960)

Diana Dors – 'Roller Coaster Blues' (1960)

Jeri Southern – 'Run' (1960)

The Barry Sisters – 'Why Don't You Do Right?' (1960)

Lynn Cornell – 'Demon Lover' (1960)

The Knightsbridge Chorale – 'Make Mine Mink' (1960)

Eric Winstone Orchestra – 'Piccadilly Third Stop' (1960)

Joe Loss – 'Wheels (Cha Cha)' (1961)

Elke Sommer – 'Be Not Notty' (1961)

Toni Eden – 'Send Me' (1961)

Matt Monro – 'My Kind of Girl' (1961)

The Beverley Sisters – 'The Sphinx Won't Tell' (1961)

Beryl Bryden – 'Moanin'' (1962)

Anita Lindblom – 'Mr Big Wheel' (1962)

Marion Ryan – 'An Occasional Man' (1962)

Kenny Ball – 'March of the Siamese Children' (1962)

Kathy Kirby – 'Dance On' (1963)

Miss X – 'Christine' (1963)

Mandy Rice-Davies – 'Close your Eyes' (1964)

Georgie Fame – 'Yeh, Yeh' (1964)

Petula Clark – 'Downtown' (1965)

Ted Heath – 'Theme from "A Summer Place"' (1965)

IV

CATALOGUE

RONALD COBB

Ronald Cobb (1909–97) is surely one of the most underrated costume designers of his generation. He entered show business as an actor, starring in a variety of noteworthy plays that included R.C. Sheriff's *Journey's End* (1930) and John Galsworthy's *Escape* (1932). In 1933, Cobb produced, wrote and acted in *Saturday to Monday*, a comedy play that heralded a change in his professional career, since he also designed the sets and costumes. His talent for costume design soon eclipsed his acting ambitions.

Throughout the Second World War, during his first marriage to the pioneering BBC sound archivist Marie Slocombe, Cobb worked as a designer for many light-hearted ENSA revues. The post-war period, however, saw him design some of the most sensational costumes ever seen in London's nightclubs. He worked for Murray's Cabaret Club between 1946 and the early 1960s.

The 'Limehouse Blues' Number

This 1946 floorshow number was perhaps the best-known in Murray's Cabaret Club's history – it was still being performed into the 1960s – and it was probably Ronald Cobb's first commission. 'Even if you have seen it before,' wrote *The Stage*'s Peter Hepple, who had confessed to watching it twenty times, 'it is still worth seeing again.'[41]

'Limehouse Blues' originally starred Laurel Grey as a waif, dancing outside a brothel in Chinatown's underworld. Amongst the crime-ridden slums of Limehouse, she danced a duet with a Chinese admirer, played by Barry Keen – one of the few men to perform in a Murray's floorshow. The number was produced by Leslie Roberts, who later established his own dance company, becoming a successful choreographer for *The Benny Hill Show*, *The Ken Dodd Show* and many other television programmes. The scene was based on the eponymous song, which evoked the atmosphere of London's Chinatown district, made famous in the 1920s by Gertrude Lawrence – who had debuted at Jack May's original Murray's Club – in the West End revue *A to Z*. Just as important a source of inspiration was the film *Ziegfeld Follies*, released the same year as the floorshow. Vincente Minnelli directed a segment of the film entitled 'Limehouse

Blues', a fantasy dance sequence that featured Fred Astaire as a poverty-stricken Chinese labourer who attempts to woo a glamorous Chinese woman, played by Lucille Bremer.

Just how closely Ronald Cobb's vision was implemented by the seamstresses can be seen when comparing his designs for this number (**pp.106–09**) with a rare photograph of a performance in 1946 (**p.82**). The costumes are all bold contours and sleek lines. They strongly resemble those worn by Hollywood superstar Anna May Wong and actor George Raft in *Limehouse Blues* – yet another film, produced in 1934, that dramatised the song's lyrics.

The Latin Craze

Riffing on the exoticism of Chinatown's seedy underworld gave audiences what they wanted – a fantastical image of cultures generally foreign to Percival Murray's customers. Murray's Cabaret Club exploited this penchant for the 'other' in countless floorshow numbers based around the theme of Latin America. Ronald Cobb executed many such designs (**p.110–12**) in the early 1950s, when the Latin dance craze was at its height in London's night-clubs. British dance band music – once the rage in the 1920s and 1930s – was declining year by year, only to be replaced by rock music in the latter part of the decade. Nightlife revellers could hardly dance to American crooners like Frank Sinatra or Dean Martin, who were consistently topping the UK charts, let alone the increasingly dated swooning of Britain's Anne Shelton or Dickie Valentine.

Latin music in the form of Perez Prado's mambos and Carmen Miranda's sambas filled this dance music void and were a staple of the Murray's repertoire. One of Cobb's costume designs on this theme (**p.113**) was so successful that it has become the most famous image to be associated with Murray's Cabaret Club; it appeared on many of its programmes, souvenir brochures and advertising leaflets for years afterwards.

Ronald Cobb outside the club, with his wife, the pioneering BBC sound archivist Marie Slocombe (left) and her sister, Edna, a well-known ballet teacher.
1940s
© Rick Dalgleish

Advertising poster from the 1950s, incorporating a costume design by Ronald Cobb. The photograph below reveals showgirls wearing similar costumes in a Latin floorshow at Murray's.
c.1965
© Victoria & Albert Museum

Murray's
Cabaret Club

LONDON'S OLDEST LUXURY
NIGHT CLUB

★

7.30 p.m. – 3 a.m.
DINNER, DANCING

★

BEAK STREET
REGENT STREET
LONDON, W.1

GERrard 4623, 3241, 6862

LONDON'S
TWO LARGEST
FLOOR SHOWS
(10 p.m. and 1 a.m.)

The 'Brazilian Bombshell' Carmen Miranda popularised Latin music. Her signature fruit hat was a feature of numerous showgirl costumes for Murray's Cabaret Club.
1941
© Pictorial Press/ Alamy

The 'Black Market' Number

For all the gaiety beneath Beak Street, London in the post-war period was a pretty drab city. Various restrictions during and after the war prompted a huge black market trade in which petty criminals who dealt in rationed goods profiteered. These 'spivs' were parodied in London's theatres – by the comedian Arthur English, for example, who did a famous spiv routine at the Windmill Theatre. Likewise, Ronald Cobb executed costume designs for a spiv for Murray's Cabaret Club. Rather than ignore the economic realities of the careworn metropolis, Percival Murray's floorshow producer, Leslie Roberts, satirised them for entertainment value when he devised the 'Black Market' number in 1948.

One of Ronald Cobb's designs for this number (**p.114**) creatively references rationing and coupons. Another – a capitalist witch (**p.115**) – shows a lady smothered in banknotes. At one point, showgirls dressed as mechanics about to change some Dunlop tyres danced to 'Get Out and Get Under (to Fix Up his Automobile)' (**p.115**). It was a clever move as that year saw the return of the International Motor Show to London's Earl's Court after years of wartime abeyance. The enormously successful 1948 Motor Show was an automotive spectacle the like of which would never be witnessed again. For the next two decades, the event was one of the most important in Percival Murray's calendar, prompting businessmen to flock to his nightclub. According to one visitor to Murray's, 'waiters' pockets bulge with larger tips,

the popping of champagne corks is a veritable barrage, [and] bands seem to play a little louder.'[42] Sir Patrick Hennessy, then Chairman of Ford, even reported that they sold more cars at Murray's than at the Motor Show itself.[43]

Glamour

Whether strutting the fashions of Fifth Avenue (**p.116**) or donning the garb of 'Gay Paree' (**p.117**), Ronald Cobb's ladies ooze sophistication. Many (**pp.117–18**) look like glamorous Horst models from *Vogue* magazine in the 1950s. Others (**pp.119–21**) are reminiscent of Cecil Beaton's costumes for the Ascot scene in *My Fair Lady* (though they in fact predate them). Cobb sprinkled these designs

Left: **Ronald Cobb's costume design for a spiv.** **late 1940s/early 1950s** © Mary Evans Picture Library

Right: **Showgirls wearing Ronald Cobb's costumes at Murray's Cabaret Club.** **1954** © *The Sketch/ Illustrated London News*

with glitter and pasted on silver foil so they still sparkle when they catch the light – almost seventy years after they were executed. A group of showgirls wearing Cobb's creations (**p.122**) in a 1954 photograph look like a cross between debutantes at some Mayfair ball and ballerinas relaxing backstage after dancing *Swan Lake* at Covent Garden. The age of the debutante was still alive and well when this photograph was taken. Just as striking are Ronald Cobb's more casual cocktail dress fashions (**p.124**).

Fashion
photographs by
Horst P. Horst for
Vogue.
1950 (a) and 1953
(b)
© Horst P. Horst/
Condé Nast/Getty

Kinky Visions

As risqué as they are glamorous, Ronald Cobb's illustrations blend style with erotica, suggesting a sort of keyhole voyeurism (**p.125**). Diana Melly, wife of the singer and raconteur George Melly, nostalgically remembers Ronald Cobb's creations for her. She was only 16 when she told her mother that she was starring as a nurse in the 'London Town' number at Murray's in 1953. What she didn't tell her mother was that the nurse was a particularly sexy one, envisaged by Ronald Cobb in his design as posing suggestively with a hypodermic syringe (**p.128**). Nor did Diana tell her mother of her role as Cupid (**p.127**) in the 'Wedding' number:

> I had to flit across the floor, pointing my bow and arrow at the bride (**p.126**) and groom, do a few twirls, then stand very still at the back of the stage and whip my bra off while the curtains closed to hide my skinny body from the audience.[44]

Such kitsch fantasies wove their way into Cobb's other designs, in the form of teasing air stewardesses, stern-stockinged policewomen, naughty Bo Peeps and startled Red Riding Hoods (**pp.128–32**). They also served as proto-types for the racy illustrations that Ronald Cobb provided for porn baron Paul Raymond's *Penthouse* and *Mayfair* magazines in the late 1960s; the original designs for the latter sold for thousands of pounds in 2009 at Christie's.

Space

In 1954, the prolific film producers Edward and Harry Danziger asked Ronald Cobb to devise costumes for their new movie, *Devil Girl from Mars*. This cult classic came out at a time that saw a spate of enthusiasm for science fiction movies, such as *The Day the Earth Stood Still* (1951). Cobb went on to design costumes for Murray's that drew on this campy space-age aesthetic. One of these (**p.133**), also dating from 1954, transforms its showgirl into a sort of cosmic dominatrix, much in the same vein as Nyah, the female alien commander from Mars in the Danziger film. A photograph of a showgirl wearing the costume in a 1955 performance shows how Cobb's dress – the design for which he used silver foil – gleamed under the spotlights. Like his costume for Nyah, Cobb's showgirl costume is futuristic and classy, though the dark lipstick, spiked headdress, silver arm bangles, arabesque bra, veil and black dress place her firmly in S&M territory. The same can be seen in Cobb's other space age designs where we find batgirls with chokers and galactic queens donning red capes (**p.134**). It is little surprise, therefore, that Ronald Cobb was asked in 1971 to design the costumes for *The Avengers*, a play based on the popular television series, staged at the Prince of Wales theatre, and starring Sue Lloyd, Jeremy Lloyd, Simon Oates and Kate O'Mara.

Showgirls Paulette Wedgbury (with maracas) and Beryl Keen (with drum) wearing Ronald Cobb's costumes.
1955
© *The Sketch/ Illustrated London News*

Nyah, played by Patricia Laffan, in *The Devil Girl from Mars*. 1954
© Ron Burton/ Hulton/Getty

Showgirls in space-age costumes. c.1958
© Chronicle/ Alamy/Trinity Mirror/ Findmypast Newspaper Archive

A Bizarre Imagination

Ronald Cobb's 'bizarre imagination', it was once said, 'is responsible for some of the most unusual garments ever seen'.[45] Lest it be thought that his chandelier-wearing lady was merely a playful sketch (**p.135**), a photograph of one of the showgirls wearing it proves that nothing was too daring for Percival Murray's seamstresses. This combination of ingenuity and style found its way into Cobb's unusually creative G-strings, which often incorporated sexual puns – from a fan to a violin (G-string) or a heart (**pp.136–37**). Cobb integrated these features by altering the mechanics of the G-string in order to devise a new construction called the 'C-string', which dispensed with side fastenings.

'Seasonal Charms'

This floorshow, based on the seasons of the year and performed from 1962 onwards, was likely the last for which Ronald Cobb designed. Only his sketches for the first number, 'April Showers', exist (**pp.138–40**). This number was particularly successful because of its special effects – at one point, hundreds of bubbles imitating rain cascaded down from the ceiling. Pathé film footage from 1962 shows comedian Fred Emney arriving at the club in a car crammed full of showgirls, one of whom appears to be Christine Keeler. They are seen entering the club before the footage cuts to a segment of 'April Showers', performed for an audience that includes debonair actor Terence Alexander cosying up to a young blonde companion. The costumes for the 'Summer' number can be seen in a 1962 publicity shoot of the showgirls on a Sussex beach. The final number in the floorshow was called 'Winter Wonderland', for which the costume bill apparently ran into thousands of pounds. Again, surviving Pathé footage records the entire number, revealing showgirls clad in white fur, snug hoods and diamante necklaces. What follows is an amusingly twee display of prancing reindeer and twinkling icicles.

Ronald Cobb is not unknown in the art world. His work does come up for auction, albeit infrequently, and the V&A holds a selection of his costume designs for the Eve Club, Percival Murray's nightclub rival. The Eve opened in 1953 and brazenly imitated the style of entertainment offered by Murray's, probably because Elena Constantinescu and Jimmy O'Brien, its founders, were ex-Murray's employees. They poached Cobb from Murray's to design their floorshows, and he even ended up marrying the Eve's star dancer, Sheila Douglas-Pennant, as his second wife. The upshot is that only Ronald Cobb's later work for the Eve has come to be appreciated – yet few of those designs are anything like as effective as those he executed for Percival Murray.

The 'Winter Wonderland' floorshow. The spectacularly dressed leading lady, Noelle Christy (bottom still) wears a heavily embroidered ice-blue satin gown, embellished with rhinestones and trimmed with twenty white fox skins.
1962
© British Pathé

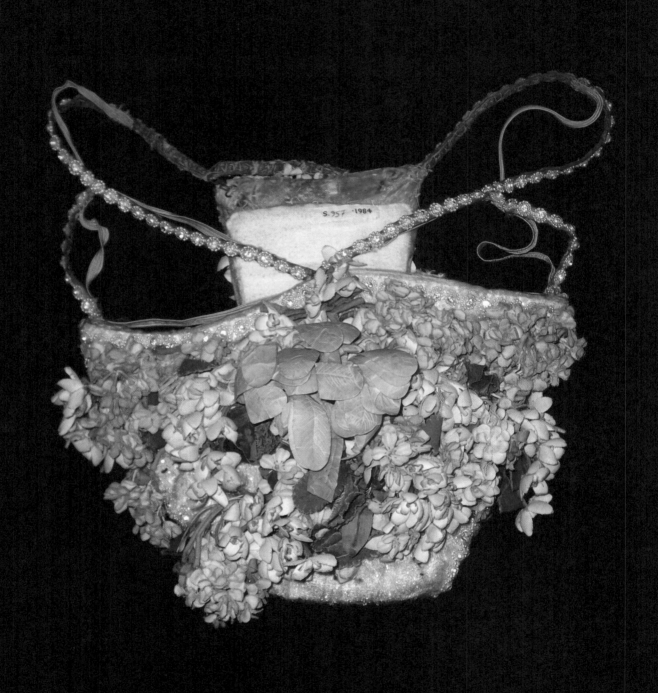

The 'April Showers' floorshow number. The G-string worn by the principal dancer is now in the V&A. It is made of white velvet, covered in fleece, edged with diamante and decorated with fabric spring flowers. 1962
© British Pathé / Victoria & Albert Museum

1

2

3

COBB 46.

5

6

7

8

9

10

11

14

15

16

17

18

19

20

21

22

23

24

25

26

27

28

29

30

31

32

33

34

35

36

37

38

39

40

41

42

52.

43

44   45

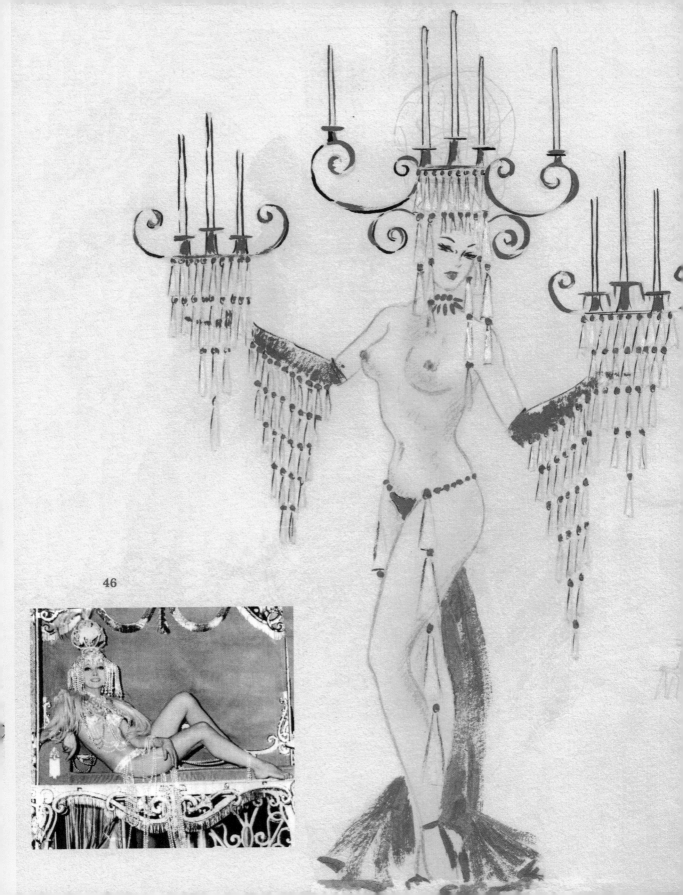

46

47

48

49

50

51

52

53

54

55

BLACK MARKET NO.

3 WITCHES

56

57

58

60

61

62

63

MICHAEL BRONZE

Michael Bronze (1916–79), born Maurice Hatzfeld, was associated with Murray's Cabaret Club from 1939 until the mid-1960s. During that period, he also executed costume designs for many West End productions – particularly musical revues and pantomimes – and was one of the costume designers for the Windmill Theatre. Good examples of his work can be found in the V&A, particularly his 1960s costumes for the 'Holiday on Ice' theatrical shows, both in the UK and on the Continent.

'Vamps Through The Ages'

This was Michael Bronze's first commission for a Murray's floorshow and is the earliest known show performed at the club, in 1939. The showgirls were photographed in their costumes for this number by *The Tatler* and *The Sketch*. 'A fine programme of loveliness and grace', the show took the form of a parade of femmes fatales (**pp.166–67**).[46] Cleopatra, complete with an asp slithering over her breasts, was the lead (**p.167**). Bronze's style is similar to that of the Victorian artist Aubrey Beardsley. In fact, his costume design for 'Salome' (**p.168**) is comparable to Beardsley's own illustrations of the character in the eponymous play by Oscar Wilde. Bronze's designs, however, were clearly not treated with the hallowed respect commanded by a work of art; someone has scrawled the telephone number of Murray's Cabaret Club over his design for 'Miss Cabaret 1940' (**p.169**).

**Michael Bronze in
his studio.**
1956
© Cabaret Girl/
British Film
Institute

**Showgirls wearing
Michael Bronze's
creations for
the 'Vamps
Through the Ages'
floorshow.**
1939
© The Sketch/
Illustrated London
News

'The Stomach Dance', an illustration by Aubrey Beardsley for Oscar Wilde's *Salome*.
1894
© Mary Evans Picture Library

'Enchantment'

Michael Bronze didn't work for Percival Murray again until the mid-1950s, when he designed the costumes for a number called 'Enchantment' in 1956. Fortunately, a segment of this routine was filmed for the *Cabaret Girl* documentary that year, and this has made it possible to identify which designs were worn for the show, and what they eventually looked like. This number was essentially an eccentric fashion show of spectacular fur-based costumes, with a bill running to over £7,000 in 1956 (almost £230,000 today). 'Thousands of pounds worth of fashionable furs,' remarks the commentator in the documentary, 'wrapped round a million pounds worth of gorgeous girl.'[47]

The footage reveals a glittering scene of smartly dressed couples seated at tables, watching a pageant of showgirls who step forward in turn to show off their dresses. A singer praises the beauty of each costume with an accent of exaggerated Received Pronunciation, much-favoured by London's nightclub soubrettes in the 1950s. The first costume is of a 'Persian cat', followed by:

White fox, the warmest from the Arctic;
The most cuddlesome of furs.
This lovely fur as white as a snowball,
As soft as a snowflake,
The envy of all!

Ranch mink fashioned with an Oriental slant,
But Eastern or Western the ladies adore it.
Such riches, such splendour,
The beauty it lends her,
A fur that makes Madam supreme.
Mink will make Madam, Oh dream!

Leopard captured from the jungle,
Fashioned with live lions of the feminine form.
This savage fur tamed for her pleasure,
As smooth as her shoulders,
The jungle's treasure!

And finally, sapphire mink;
The costliest of them all.
A fur for the favoured few,
The finest, the rarest,
It's meant for the fairest.
Mink for London's elite,
Sapphire makes Madam complete!

'Enchantment', the floorshow with costume designs by Michael Bronze. Shown in the top still are (left to right) the white fox, the Persian cat and *'Ranch mink fashioned with an Oriental slant'*. The bottom still shows the leading lady in sapphire mink. 1956

© *Cabaret Girl/* British Film Institute

Showgirls in Michael Bronze's 'Enchantment'. The crinoline costumes comprised stylised bow ties, tutus and bras, all decorated with gold rosettes and diamante. 1956
© Cabaret Girl/ British Film Institute

At this point the chorus of showgirls, wearing elegantly bejewelled costumes, breaks into dance and sings a song called 'Take Back Your Cadillac', by Murray's then-bandleader, Don Lorusso. Michael Bronze's designs for the Persian cat (**p.170**), the white fox (**p.171**), the Oriental mink (**p.172**), the leopard (**p.173**) and the sapphire mink (**pp.174–75**) complement his equally lavish costumes for the chorus (**pp.176–78**).

That the costumes are so formal in comparison with Ronald Cobb's is unsurprising; in addition to being a theatrical costumier, Michael Bronze was also a dress designer for London's high society, doing everything from debutante gowns to haute-couture for aristocratic ladies. That said, Bronze's costumes do share Ronald Cobb's penchant for space-age glamour, albeit blended with the style of Norman Hartnell and graced in sweeping mink coats (**pp.179–80**).

'Leopard captured from the jungle': Doro George wears Michael Bronze's fabulous leopard costume for 'Enchantment'. She is seen in the foreground of the still (bottom). 1956
© The Sketch/ Illustrated London News/Cabaret Girl/British Film Institute

'Midsummer Melody'

A costume for 'Midsummer Melody', today looking sad and neglected. The flower-shaped bra and elaborate headdress are made from silk, velvet, wire and elastic.
c.1956
© Victoria & Albert Museum

This was the number performed after 'Enchantment' in the new 1956 floor-show. 'Expertly produced, excellently lit, and beautifully dressed', was the verdict in *The Stage*.[48] Yet this number was never filmed and few photographs of the costumes survive outside of those in souvenir programmes. The costumes were based around the theme of flowers and weeds (**pp.181–83**) and many have recently been identified in the V&A's collection.

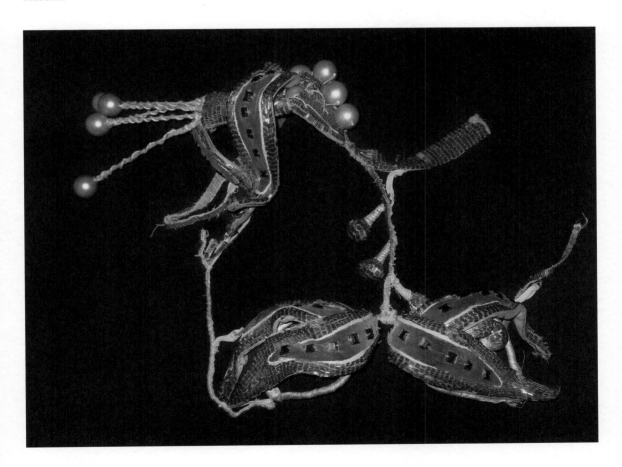

This headdress for 'Midsummer Melody' is covered in thousands of bugle beads. It is extraordinarily heavy, though never slipped from the showgirls' heads because the beading was perfectly balanced throughout.
c.1956
© Victoria & Albert Museum/ The Stage Media Company Limited

'The Big Top'

This number entered the repertoire in 1958, where it remained for several
years. It was a bold, brassy event-packed Big Top scene, complete with flash-
ing coloured lights, rope twirlers and showgirls dressed as clowns and circus
animals. Although no film footage survives, an impressive double-spread
colour photograph in one of the souvenir programmes shows the whole
company posed in a highly staged shot, wearing all the costumes. Michael
Bronze's designs for 'The Big Top' (**pp.183–88**) include one particularly unusual costume that covered its wearer with doves (**p.189**). Pathé footage from
1961 shows this costume's headdress being modelled in Elsie Burchmore's
workshop. It was in fact Christine Keeler who sported this dress in 1961, when
she starred in the show.

'Arabian Rhapsody'

The only other known photograph of Christine Keeler in a Murray's costume was taken by Kenneth Bandy, and shows her wearing Michael Bronze's costume for the 'Arabian Rhapsody' floorshow (**p.190**). There is Pathé footage from 1961 of the girls dancing this routine, dressed as harem inmates and Sultans. They wave scimitars and wear exquisitely beaded dresses, decorated with bangles, beads and baubles. If you squint at the grainy footage, a girl resembling Christine Keeler wearing the same costume as in the

photograph dances in the back row. 'The girls just seem to appear en masse from some hidden supply,' marvelled Reg Barlow of *The Stage*'s 'Nightbeat' column. Though he confessed to 'a weakness for hordes of pretty girls', the costumes were in his estimation 'just too fabulous for words – and "fabulous" is a word normally absent from my vocabulary'. [49]

The construction of Michael Bronze's costume designs for this number (**pp.191–95**) has also been caught on film, showing Elsie Burchmore directing her seamstresses in the workshop on Percival Murray's estate. Though the footage is silent, Elsie appears to instruct a seamstress as to how she would like one of these fantastic headdresses to be ornamented. Photographs exist too of various dancers sporting their costumes for this number; amazingly, and luckily, it has been possible to identify the fate of the corresponding costumes through online auction sites.

Left: **Christine Keeler wearing Michael Bronze's costume for 'Arabian Rhapsody'.** c.1961 © Kenneth Bandy/ Mayor Gallery/ James Birch

Elsie Burchmore demonstrating how to bead an elaborate headdress for 'Arabian Rhapsody'. 1961 © British Pathé

Left: **This velvet costume, worn in the 'Arabian Rhapsody' number, was sold on eBay in 2017 for over £200. Photographs in newspapers make it possible to identify it as having been worn by Patti Dalton. Early 1960s**
© Costume Sales Room/eBay

Above and right: **Two heavy headdresses of velvet, silver tissue, jewels and feathers, that appeared on eBay in 2017. They were soiled with make-up marks on the inside when sold. The one on the right creatively combines the style of the sultan's harem with a futuristic space-age look. Early 1960s**
© Costume Sales Room/eBay

'Witchcraft'

This was perhaps the most impressive floorshow designed by Michael Bronze. Riveting Pathé footage shows an amazingly large cast crammed into the tiny space. 'How they achieve so much on this small stage is something of a miracle,' wrote Reg Barlow, once again reporting on his favourite nightspot:

> Smoke billows through the glass flooring ... as witches cast their spells, cackle their mumbo-jumbo, and tend their potent brew. Skeleton skifflers take the floor, and a wicked blonde with horns pushing her halo aside leads other lasses in an ostentatious display of strutting and diamond flashing – the whole scene is charged with symbolism.[50]

Skeletons and witches vie with devils and angels (**pp.197–99**). Amongst this macabre spectacle, three lead showgirls draped in diamonds and fur purr the lines, 'I don't want to be a goody-goody; I just want to be a nasty, naughty girl!'[51] One of the witches 'came right up to my table and dropped a miniature bottle of brandy into my lap', testified another overexcited journalist. 'It was probably to steady my nerves.'[52] Once again, a handful of costumes worn in this number have appeared in online auctions, and a particularly lavish headdress from the routine is even on permanent display in the V&A's Theatre and Performance galleries.

Whereas Ronald Cobb's Deco girls tease and titillate, Michael Bronze's lithe vamps are more overtly sexual. Cobb's girls are generally covered up, but Michael Bronze's often have their breasts exposed. The final costumes, however, were not always so revealing; Elsie Burchmore's seamstresses tended to cover up bare breasts for the sake of decency. It is just possible, therefore, that all this nudity in Bronze's sketches was a joke on his part – a way of poking fun at their apparent formality. Or maybe they were always more than functional costume designs – fantastical visions, perhaps, of their designer, who intricately rendered his seductresses in the mischievous manner of Aubrey Beardsley.

Devils (top) and
angels (bottom)
in 'Witchcraft'
1961
© British Pathé

Leading ladies
Ann Griffin,
Noelle Christy
and Dilys
Rowlands (left
to right) in
'Witchcraft'.
1961
© British Pathé

The champagne
bucket headdress
is on display in
the V&A. It is
made of gold
lamé encrusted
with rhinestones,
feathers and
sequins.
1961
© British Pathé/
Victoria & Albert
Museum

Right: **A devilish red velvet headdress, worn in Michael Bronze's 'Witchcraft' number. Early 1960s** © Costume Sales Room/eBay

64

NELL Guy

65

66

67

MISS CABARET 1940.
GERRARD 4623

69

Michael BRONZE

70

Michael Bronze

71

72

Michael Bronze

73

SAPPHIRE MINK

20 yards

74

75

76

Michael Bronze

77

Michael Bronz

Black grosgrain
green Satin

78

Black

79

80

81

82

83

84

85

86

87

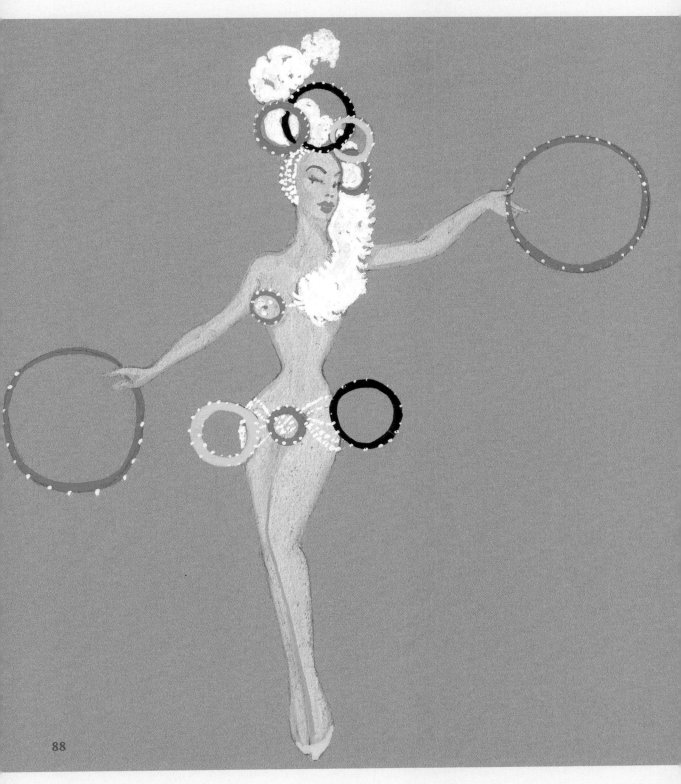

89

90

91

92

93

94

95

96

97

98

99

B'd

100

101

103

104

105

106

OTHER DESIGNERS

Ronald Cobb and Michael Bronze were responsible for the majority, and the best, of the costumes at Murray's Cabaret Club; their work makes up the bulk of Elsie Burchmore's collection. However, Percival Murray also engaged other interesting and varied designers throughout the club's history.

Hilda Wetton (1896–1980) was a legendary costume designer with the Windmill Theatre, working there with its earliest 'Revudeville' shows from 1932 onwards. She was first married to Horatio Taylor, an actor, director and scenery designer who also worked at the Windmill. In the late 1930s, she left him for the Windmill's chief set designer, Cyril Denny. Her work for the Windmill can now be seen in the V&A. Wetton's costumes for Murray's Cabaret Club probably date from the 1940s.

Her designs are immediately recognisable from their showgirls' long eye-lashes, rouged lips and coy expressions. She executed a series of designs for a floorshow devised by Laurel Grey that was based on a fan dance (**pp.208–09**). Wetton was the ideal person for the job because of her work for the Windmill, the theatre that made the fan dance famous in Britain. Censorship laws did not permit nudes to move on stage, though the Windmill dodged the rules; its nude dancers could remain within the law, so long as they stayed covered while manipulating a set of huge ostrich feather fans. The dance, therefore, required considerable skill – an ability to titillate though never reveal all.

Christine Welsford performing a typical fan dance at the Windmill Theatre. c.1950 © Keystone/Alamy

Murray's Cabaret Club had already staged performances of fan dances; in 1939, *The Tatler* reported that Denise Vane, 'England's most sensational fan-dancer', was performing there.[53] In the accompanying photograph, Denise wears a costume very similar to those in Hilda Wetton's dainty sketches for Laurel Grey's fan dance number.

Wetton worked on other Murray's shows too. Her sketches include some exquisite costumes for a 'Mexican number' (**p.210**), a leggy pirate (**p.211**), a harem girl (**p.211**), a naughty nurse (**p.212**) and a sexy milkmaid (**p.212**).

'**Dexter**' was the pseudonym of an anonymous costume designer for Murray's Cabaret Club. Nothing is known about his or her identity, though numerous sketches by Dexter exist for floorshows performed in the mid-1950s.

A handful relate to the 'Wild West' number dating from 1954 (**pp.213–15**). They are copiously annotated, as all Dexter's designs are, with instructions as to fabrics, colours, props and other accoutrements. The designs consist of an assortment of 'Diamond Lils' and 'Injun Braves'.

Dexter also worked on a floorshow number called 'Jewels', produced in 1956. Its tagline was: 'The Fantasy of a Little Boy's Dream'. It was probably Percival Murray's fantasy too – the 1956 documentary film *Cabaret Girl* shows the

Above, left: **Fan dancer Denise Vane at the club. 1939**
© *The Sketch/ Illustrated London News*

Hilda Wetton designing a costume in the Windmill Theatre. c.1934
© British Pathé

impresario, looking like a cross between Winston Churchill and Lew Grade, bursting abruptly into the fitting rooms of his country home to inspect the costumes of his half-naked showgirls. These outfits match Dexter's designs for 'Jewels'. The costumes shown on-screen are presumably also the stuff of the Little Boy's dreams: they are sea creatures based on the colour of various jewels – diamond seadragons (**p.215**), ruby jellyfish (**p.217**) and pearl lobsters (**p.218**). Percival Murray, sporting a broad grin, is next seen fiddling with these dresses, ostensibly to ensure their sturdiness, whilst the film's commentator explains that, 'The customers will forgive anything slipping ... except the boss.'[54]

'Caribbean Voodoo' is the only floorshow number the entirety of which – sound and vision – was filmed. Dating from 1956, this 'Exotic Presentation based on the Mambo' was caught on camera in the *Cabaret Girl* documentary. Its high-octane energy makes it a riveting spectacle. The showgirls twirl to a groovy Hammond organ in costumes inspired by the Caribbean (**pp.219–20**). One of them – a lavish affair with an enormous fruit basket headdress (**p.221**) – is seen earlier on, in the process of construction. To a frenzied mambo, the girls whirl around a monolithic pillar that stands in the centre of the dance floor; it was famously a bane to every choreographer who passed through Murray's, since it couldn't be moved; it was apparently holding up the building! The show still mesmerises, even if the tremendously camp dancing was also restricted by an enormous lighting system hovering overhead and an audience packed in on all sides.

Showgirls posing
for a publicity
photoshoot in
Cabaret Girl,
wearing their
costumes for
'Jewels'.
1956
© *Cabaret Girl* /
British Film
Institute

The 'Caribbean
Voodoo'
floorshow.
1956
© *Cabaret Girl* /
British Film
Institute

Seamstresses
making
headdresses
for 'Caribbean
Voodoo', and
(below) showgirls
trying them
on in Percival
Murray's home.
1956
© *Cabaret Girl/*
British Film
Institute

Virginia Dawn (1905–93) was an artist, fashion designer and cabaret chanteuse. Her real name was the colourful Suzanne Louise Virginia Duclos Sarraute McClay Dawn. Little is known about her work for Murray's Cabaret Club.

She designed a handful of extravagant costumes with an unusual take on historical revivalism, running the gamut from medieval- to eighteenth-century-inspired dress (**pp.222–24**). Dawn was French, hailing from a grand, aristocratic family, and so it is unsurprising to find a nod to the fashions of Louis XIV and seventeenth-century Versailles amongst her sketches.

Her designs are meticulously annotated, including notes as to how a certain brocade effect can be achieved in one particular

Virginia Dawn, costume designer and chanteuse. 1941
© British Pathé

sketch of a medieval noblewoman wearing an enormous chastity belt (**p.225**). It is possible that these regal designs were for a 'Coronation' number produced in 1953. The show obviously captured the zeitgeist of enthusiasm for anything coronation-inspired in the year of Elizabeth II's crowning.

Other designs relate to the 1954 'Wild West' floorshow number, for which she executed costumes for the cowgirls (**pp.226–27**). This was likely her last piece of work for Percival Murray, since she left England for America soon afterwards. She subsequently led a glamorous life as a society hostess in New York and Hollywood, where she associated with Noël Coward, Ernest Hemingway and Cole Porter.

Percival Murray (1898–1979) took a more active role in costuming his showgirls in the club's final decade. His involvement in the art direction was, in fact, never insignificant; as surviving film footage shows, he had always maintained a close connection with both his designers and the wardrobe mistress Elsie Burchmore. However, as far as devising the costumes went, Percival

Above: **Noelle Christy sporting her top-hat-and-tails worn in Percival Murray's 'Roaring Twenties' floorshow. c.1964** © Victoria & Albert Museum

Above, right: **Percival Murray 1960s**

Murray had never made more than slight modifications to what his designers had produced.

A handful of costume designs by Percival Murray do exist (**pp.228–31**), though it is unknown how many were executed, or whether they were simply recommendations in the form of preparatory sketches for Burchmore or the costume designers. Most resemble 1920s flappers, so it is possible that they were the costume designs for a floorshow first performed in 1961, called 'Percival Murray's Memories of the Twenties'. This starred a large cast, 'all of whom,' wrote one reporter, 'would appear to be wearing a king's ransom in costumes ... one example being £2,000 worth of wigs, made specially in Paris to match cuttings of the girls' hair'.[55]

Percival Murray had been involved in nightlife entertainment through-out the 1920s, so it was appropriate that this nostalgic show was stamped with his personal touch. After dancing the Charleston, the entire company of forty or so performers was spectacularly bedecked in a top-hat-and-tails finale (**p.231**).

108

109

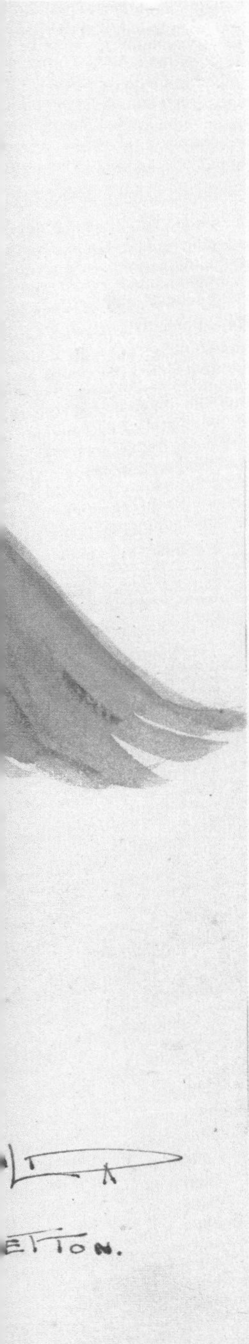
ETTON.

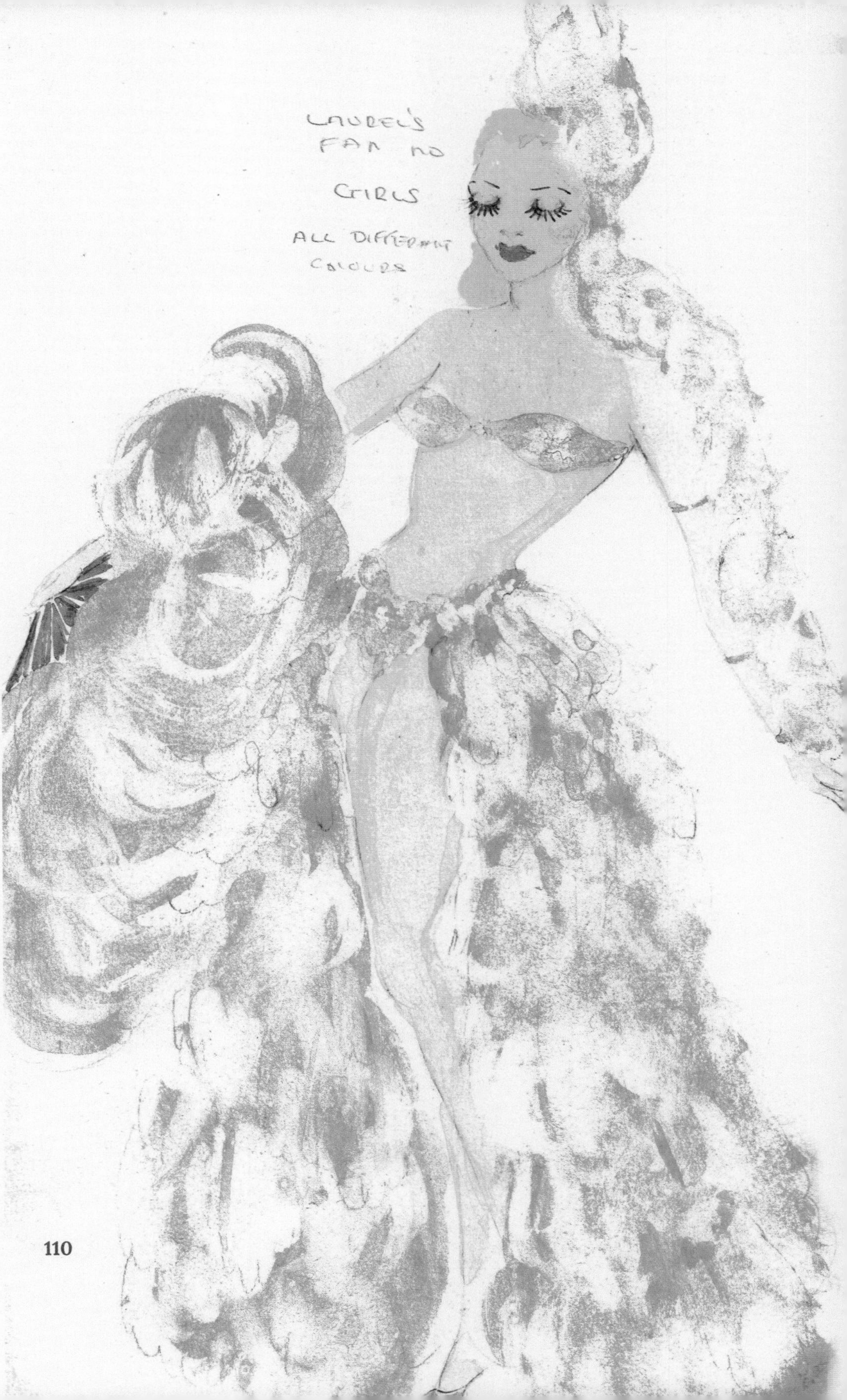
LAUREL'S
FAN NO
GIRLS
ALL DIFFERENT
COLOURS

111

112

113

114

115

116

Black velv
White sat
R64 1" #1.
4 Dg
2 Day
Green ✓
Green ✓
Black =
Black
Georget
Feather

DORO

117

118

119

INDIAN BRAVES

120

4 yards white Felt
1 yard green turquoise
1 yard orange
1 yard yellow
1 yard black
½ yard cerise

TERRY

CHIEF

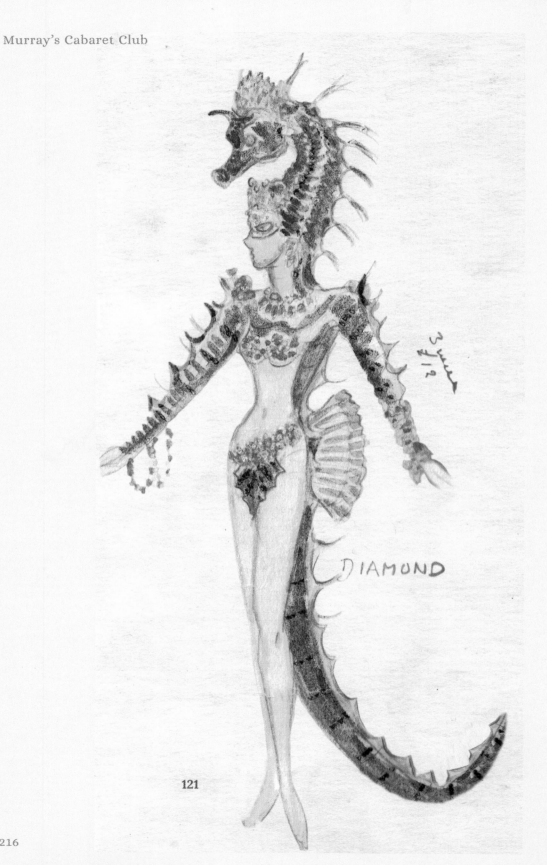

DIAMOND

121

RUBY

122

BLACK
PEARL

cape in
Blue dart
right at
silver cup

123

SHOWGIRL 3

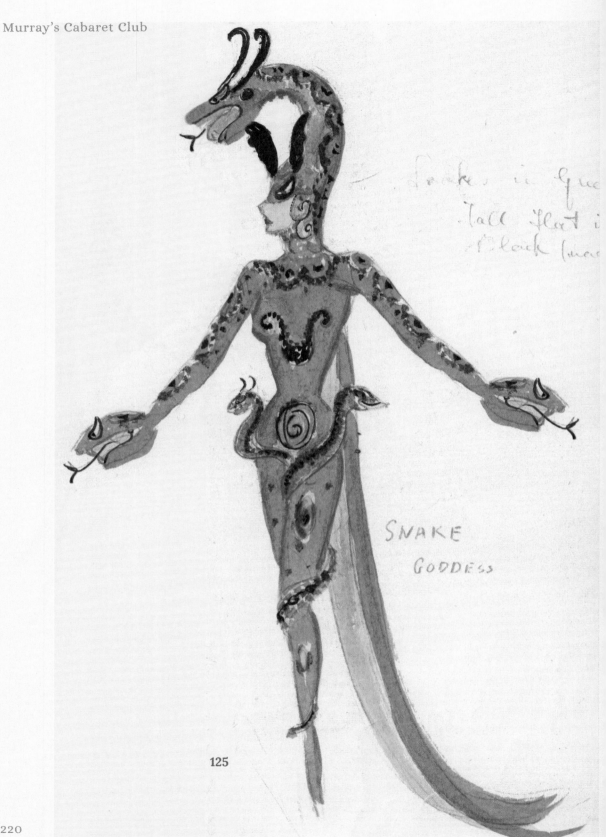

Snakes in Gree
Tall Hat i
Black hai

SNAKE
GODDESS

125

126

127

128

Late XVIII

129

Virginia Day

Mediaeval

this brocad
effect can b
obtained by
painting Re
designs on
ordinary
material

130

Virginia Da

131

132

133

134

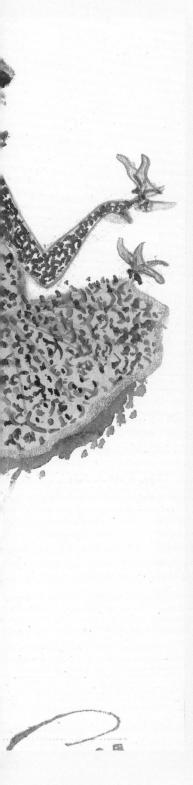

135

136

137

138

NOTES

1   Christine Keeler with Douglas Thompson, *Secrets and Lies* (London: John Blake Publishing, 2012), p.10.
2   'London's "Cabarets": First Performance at Murray's Club', *The Times*, 20 September 1922, p.8.
3   'Montmartre in London', *The Sunday Post*, 24 September 1922, p.11.
4   Percival Murray later claimed to have personally propelled Lawrence to stardom by putting her in the first ever floorshow at Jack May's Murray's Club. However, there is nothing to suggest Percival Murray worked for Murray's Club in 1920, let alone mounted a floorshow there starring Gertrude Lawrence. In any case, the intimate floorshow – as distinct from traditional cabaret – was a later innovation.
5   Ivan Patrick Gore, 'Murray's', *The Stage*, 16 February 1928, p.23.
6   Ivan Patrick Gore, 'Murray's', *The Stage*, 15 May 1930, p.12.
7   Peter Hepple, 'Nightbeat', *The Stage*, 20 December 1962, p.6.
8   Peter Hepple, 'Nightbeat', *The Stage*, 11 March 1971, p.7.
9   Paul Holt, 'Dancing at £2 a Partner Booms in the Black-Out', *Daily Express*, 17 November 1939, p.3.
10 'Trixie Scales – Warden and Croonette', *Illustrated Sporting and Dramatic News*, 31 January 1941, p.160.
11 'When it's Night-Time in London', *The Tatler*, 1 November 1939, p.161.
12 'Girl's Smile Hides Grief', *Daily Mirror*, 28 April 1941, p.8.
13 Youngman Carter, 'London Limelight', *The Tatler*, 31 March 1954, p.593.
14 Iain Crawford, 'Go Late', *The Tatler*, 20 December 1961, p.812.
15 'His Search for Showgirls', *West London Observer*, 10 September 1954, p.7.
16 'Clothes Make All the Difference', *Daily Herald*, 11 November 1955, p.7.
17 Advertisement, *The Stage*, 25 March 1971, p.18.
18 Advertisement, *The Stage*, 26 March 1964, p.16; advertisement, *The Stage*, 4 October 1956, p.14.
19 Keeler, *Secrets and Lies*, pp.2–3.
20 For example, see Advertisement, *The Stage*, 3 June 1954, p.14.
21 Peter Hepple, 'Nightbeat', *The Stage*, 11 March 1971, p.7.
22 Tony Armstrong Jones, *London* (London: Weidenfeld & Nicholson, 1958).
23 Keeler, *Secrets and Lies*, p.2.
24 Frankie Fraser with James Morton, *Mad Frank's Underworld History of Britain* (London: Random House, 2007), p.8.

24 Keeler, *Secrets and Lies*, p.2.
26 'Club Stage', *The Stage*, 26 March 1964, p.21.
27 e.g. see Advertisement, *The Stage*, 3 April 1952, p.14.
28 Keeler, *Secrets and Lies*, p.8.
29 *Ibid.*, p.2.
30 Obituary: Mandy Rice-Davies, *The Times*, 19 December 2014.
31 Christopher Ward, 'Life's Still a Cabaret', *Daily Mirror*, 19 April 1974, p.7.
32 John Viner, 'After Bunny-Day … Will London ever be the same again?', *The Tatler*, 2 July 1966, p.8.
33 Jake Arnott, *The Long Firm* (London: Sceptre, 1999).
34 Peter Hepple, 'Cabaret Time', *Theatre World* 59-60 (1963), p.79.
35 Reg Barlow, 'Nightbeat', *The Stage*, 29 October 1959, p.7.
36 'Restaurants Hit by Budget Curb on Entertainment', *The Times*, 12 October 1965, p.13.
37 Peter Hepple, 'Nightbeat', *The Stage*, 26 May 1966, p.7.
38 'William Hickey', *Daily Express*, 8 October 1975, p.9.
39 Christopher Ward, 'Life's Still a Cabaret', *Daily Mirror*, 19 April 1974, p.7.
40 Peter Hepple, 'Nightbeat', *The Stage*, 31 July 1969, p.7.
41 Peter Hepple, 'Nightbeat', *The Stage*, 23 January 1964, p.7.
42 Peter Hepple, 'Nightbeat', *The Stage*, 24 October 1963, p.7.
43 Christopher Ward, 'Life's Still a Cabaret', *Daily Mirror*, 19 April 1974, p.7.
44 Diana Melly, *Strictly Ballroom: Tales from the Dancefloor* (London: Short Books, 2015), p.60.
45 Peter Hepple, 'Nightbeat', *The Stage*, 11 March 1971, p.7.
46 'When it's Night-Time in London', *The Tatler*, 1 November 1939, p.161.
47 E.V.H. Emmett, *Cabaret Girl*, directed by Guy Blanchard (London: President Pictures, 1956).
48 R.B.M., 'Midnight Cabaret: "Moonlight and Dew"', *The Stage*, 19 December 1957, p.11.
49 Reg Barlow, 'Nightbeat', *The Stage*, 18 February 1960, p.7.
50 Reg Barlow, 'Nightbeat', *The Stage*, 15 December 1960, p.7.
51 Quoted in Reg Barlow, 'Nightbeat', *The Stage*, 12 January 1961, p.7.
52 Neville Nisse, 'Nightbeat', *The Stage*, 8 June 1961, p.7.
53 'When it's Night-Time in London', *The Tatler*, 1 November 1939, p.161.
54 E.V.H. Emmett, *Cabaret Girl*, directed by Guy Blanchard (London: President Pictures, 1956).
55 Peter Hepple, 'Nightbeat', *The Stage*, 4 June 1964, p.7.